OUR TOWN

A PLAY

IN THREE ACTS

BY

THORNTON WILDER

ACTING EDITION
Published by COWARD-MCCANN, INC.
In Cooperation with SAMUEL FRENCH, INC.

OUR TOWN

Story of the Play

In the first act the author genially outlines the history of the town, which is Grover's Corners, N. H., and something of the character of its citizens. Then he carries you into the houses of the Gibbs and Webb families, substantial homes containing substantial folks. You arrive at breakfast time and are carried through one entire day in the lives of these good people.

The second act concerns the love affair between young George Gibbs and little Emily Webb, and thus culminates in a moving wedding scene, which contains all those elements of poignant sorrow and abundant happiness that make for solemnity and impressiveness.

In the third act we are led to the cemetery on the hill, where many of the townspeople we have come to know so well are patiently and smilingly awaiting not "judgment" but greater understanding. Into their midst is led the bride, a little timid at first, a little wishful to go back to life, to live again with her memories. But she is shown how impossible, how futile it is to return. The past cannot be re-lived. Living people, humans, occupied with their petty occupations and small thoughts, know little of true joy or happiness. Truth is to be found only in the future.

SOME SUGGESTIONS FOR THE DIRECTOR

It is important to maintain a continual *dryness* of tone,—the New England understatement of sentiment, of surprise, of tragedy. A shyness about emotion. These significances are conveyed by the eyes and a sharpening and distinctness of the voice. (So in the Stage-Manager on the Civil War veterans: "All they knew was the name, friends,—the United States of America. The United States of America." And in all the dealings of the mothers with their children where a matter-of-factness overlays the concern.)

———

It has already been proven that absence of scenery does not constitute a difficulty and that the cooperative imagination of the audience is stimulated by that absence. There remain, however, two ways of producing the play. One, with a constant subtle adjustment of lights and sound effects; and one through a still bolder acknowledgment of artifice and make-believe: the rooster's crow, the train and factory whistles and school bells frankly man-made and in the spirit of "play." I am inclined to think that this latter approach, though apparently "amateurish" and rough at first, will prove the more stimulating in the end, and will prepare for the large claim on attention and imagination in the last act. The scorn of verisimilitude throws all the greater emphasis on the ideas which the play hopes to offer.

———

It seems advisable that at the opening of the play where the audience is first introduced to pantomime and imaginary props, that Mrs. Gibbs and

Mrs. Webb in the preparation of breakfast perform much of their business with their backs to the audience, and do not distract and provoke its attention with too distinct and perhaps puzzling a picture of the many operations of coffee-grinding, porridge-stirring, etc.

At the beginning of the wedding scene there is an abrupt change of approach. The audience is hearing the thoughts of the characters and is seeing a symbolical statement of attitudes which never were consciously expressed by the characters in their daily life. This change is greatly aided by the entrance of the bride and groom through the aisles of the auditorium; and by the fact that it is accompanied by the very soft singing of the hymns by the congregation. It would be well that George on arriving on the stage draws back well toward the proscenium, indicating that this scene does not literally take place in the church or before the church. After Mrs. Gibbs's line: "George! If anyone should hear you! Now stop! Why, I'm ashamed of you!" George passes his hand over his forehead, as though emerging from a dream, and with a complete change of matter, returning to realism, explains: "What? Where's Emily?" Mrs. Gibbs and George do not touch each other during the scene until she straightens his tie, and the strong emotion is indicated by tension, not by weeping. In the following scene between Emily and her father, however. Emily is in tears and flings herself into her father's arms.

The Stage-Manager-Clergyman's speech: "I've married two hundred couples in my day," etc., is not delivered to the village congregation before him, but across their heads, an almost dreamy meditation, during which the tableau on the stage "freezes."

In the last act it is important to remove from the picture of the seated dead any suggestion of the morbid or lugubrious. They sit easily; there is nothing of the fixed and unwinking about their eyes. The impression is of patient composed waiting.

Emily's revisiting her home and her farewell to the world is under strong emotion, but the emotion is that of wonder rather than of sadness. Even the "I love you all, everything!" is realization and discovery as much as it is poignancy.

T. W.

Copy of Program of the First Performance of OUR
TOWN as produced at HENRY MILLER'S THEATRE,
New York.

———

JED HARRIS

presents

OUR TOWN

A Play By

THORNTON WILDER

with

FRANK CRAVEN

Production by Mr. Harris
Technical Direction by Raymond Sovey
Costumes Designed by Helene Pons

———

THE CAST

(In the order of their appearance)

STAGE MANAGER .... *Frank Craven*
DR. GIBBS .... *Jay Fassett*
JOE CROWELL .... *Raymond Roe*
HOWIE NEWSOME .... *Tom Fadden*
MRS. GIBBS .... *Evelyn Varden*
MRS. WEBB .... *Helen Carew*
GEORGE GIBBS .... *John Craven*
REBECCA GIBBS .... *Marilyn Erskine*
WALLY WEBB .... *Charles Wiley, Jr.*
EMILY WEBB .... *Martha Scott*
PROFESSOR WILLARD .... *Arthur Allen*
MR. WEBB .... *Thomas W. Ross*

WOMAN IN THE BALCONY .... *Carrie Weller*
MAN IN THE AUDITORIUM .... *Walter O. Hill*
LADY IN THE BOX ...., ... *Aline McDermott*
SIMON STIMSON .... *Philip Coolidge*
MRS. SOAMES .... *Dore Merande*
CONSTABLE WARREN .... *E. Irving Locke*
SI CROWELL .... *Billy Redfield*

BASEBALL PLAYERS .... {
Alfred Ryder
William Roehrick
Thomas Coley
}

SAM CRAIG .... *Francis G. Cleveland*
JOE STODDARD .... *William Wadsworth*

ASSISTANT STAGE MANAGERS ..... {
Thomas Morgan
Alfred Ryder
}

PEOPLE OF THE TOWN: *Carrie Weller, Alice Donald-son, Walter O. Hill, Arthur Allen, Charles Mel-lody, Katharine Raht, Mary Elizabeth Forbes, Dor-othy Nolan, Jean Platt, Barbara Brown, Alida Stanley, Barbara Burton, Lyn Swann, Dorothy Ryan, Shirley Osborn, Emily Boileau, Ann Wes-ton, Leon Rose, John Irving Finn, Van Shem, Charles Walters, William Short, Frank Howell, Max Beck, James Malaidy, Charles Wiley, Sr.*

The entire play takes place in Grovers Corners, N.H.

OUR TOWN

ACT ONE

*As the audience assembles the curtain is up and the
stage is completely bare. A pilot light on a short
stand is lighted, down left near the proscenium.
At the appointed "curtain hour", the* STAGE MAN-
AGER *saunters from Right, a script in his hand,
a pipe in his mouth, hat on head. Crossing off
Left, he reappears with a table which he places
L. C. leaving the script on it. He then sets
chairs per the set diagram (see appendix). He
does the same for table and chairs Right, then
crosses for the prompt script, which he takes
down Right and passes it offstage to an unseen
assistant, then lounges against the proscenium.*
*During the setting of the stage a blue early-morning
light has been established, and a pinspot has
picked up the* STAGE MANAGER *as he reaches
the proscenium.* STAGE MANAGER *now looks
over the audience, puffs his pipe, consults
watch, deprecates late-comers, etc., while the
house lights gradually dim. When the house is
quiet, he speaks.*

STAGE MANAGER. This play is called "Our Town."
It was written by Thornton Wilder and produced
by ———————. In it you will see Mr. ———————,
Mr. ———————, Mr. ———————, Miss ———————,
Miss ———————, Miss ———————, and many
others too numerous to mention. The name of our
town is Grover's Corners, N. H., just over the line
from Massachusetts; latitude 42 degrees, 40 minutes, longitude 70 degrees, 37 minutes.

(*A light strip on the floor up L. starts glowing into a dawn effect, which is followed by gradual morning light, which increases to noon through the action of the act.*)

The first act shows a day in our town. The date is May 7, 1901, just before dawn. (*COCK CROW off-stage.*) Aya, just about. Sky is beginnin' to show some streaks of light over in the East there, back of our mountain. (*Xing half up C.*) The mornin' star always gets wonderful bright the minute before it has to go. (*Stares up off L. at star a moment.*) Well, now I'll show you how our town lies. (*Xing up C. into Main Street*) Up here is Main Street. Cuttin' across it over there on the left is the railroad tracks. Across the tracks is—Polish Town. You know, foreign people that come here to work in the mill, couple of Canuck families, and the Catholic Church. (*Xing few steps down, pointing off L. with pipe.*) The Congregational Church is over there; the Presbyterian's across the street. Methodist and Unitarian are over there. (*Off down R.*) Baptist is down in the holla (*out front*)—by the river. (*Xing up C. again*) Next to the Post Office there (*Off L.*) is the Town Hall; jail is in the basement. Bryan once made a speech from those steps there. (*Swinging arms along street*) Along Main Street there's a row of stores. Hitchin' posts and horse-blocks in front of 'em. (*Xing down a few steps*) First automobile's goin' to come along in about five years— belonged to Banker Cartwright, our town's richest citizen. Lives up in the big white house up there on the hill. (*Pointing with pipe off R.*) Here's the grocery store and Mr. Morgan's drug store. (*Pointing with pipe R. and L. behind him*) Most everybody in town manages to look into these stores once a day. (*Xing down C., pointing to furniture R. C.*) This is our doctor's house—Doc Gibbs'.

(*Two* ASSISTANT STAGE MANAGERS *bring trellises, with roses climbing over them, definitely worn and theatrical, from behind the tormentors, and set them at angles just below and center of the tormentors; then they withdraw behind tormentors.*)

This is the back door— (*Glances at both trellises*) Here's a couple of trellises for those that feel they have to have scenery— This is Mrs. Gibbs' garden—(*down of furniture*) corn—peas—beans—hollyhocks—heliotrope, and a lot of burdock. In those days our newspapers came out twice a week—the *Grover's Corners Sentinel*—and this (*Indicating furniture L. C., Xing L. of C.*) is Editor Webb's house. And this is Mrs. Webb's garden. (*Down of furniture L. C.*) Just like Mrs. Gibbs's, only it's got a lot of sunflowers too— Right here— (*Xing to run hands up and down an imaginary tree where the chair just L. of C. stands*) is a big butternut tree. (*He looks up at it, then faces out and Xes down C. onto apron.*) Nice town, y' know what I mean? Nobody very remarkable ever come out of it, s'far as we know. The earliest dates on the tombstones up there in the cemetery (*Off L.*) say 1670. They're Grovers and Cartwrights and Gibbses and Herseys—same names as around here now. Well, as I said, it's early morning. The only lights on in town are in a cottage over by the tracks where a Polish mother's just had twins. And in the Joe Crowell house, where Joe Junior's gettin' ready to deliver the mornin' paper. And in the depot, where Shorty Hawkins is gettin' ready to flag the 5:45 for Boston. (*TRAIN WHISTLE offstage.* STAGE MANAGER *takes watch from vest pocket and consults it.*) Aya—there she is. Naturally out in the country, all around, they've been lights on for some time, what with milkin' and so on. But town folks sleep late.

So—another day's begun. (*Looks off L.*) There's Doc Gibbs comin' down Main Street now, comin' back from that baby case.

(MRS. GIBBS, *a plump, pleasant woman in the thirties, comes downstairs R. She bustles to put up shade, open window a bit, then to make a wood fire in the stove.*)

And here's his wife comin' downstairs to get breakfast. (STAGE MANAGER *Xing down R.*) Doc Gibbs died in 1930. New hospital's named after him. Mrs. Gibbs died first—long time ago, in fact. She went out to visit her daughter Rebecca, who married an insurance man in Canton, Ohio, and died there—pneumonia—but her body was brought back here.

(MRS. GIBBS *grinds coffee into a pot above the stove.*)

She's up in the cemetery there now—in with a whole mess of Gibbses and Herseys—she was Julia Hersey before she married Dr. Gibbs in the Congregational Church over there. In our town we like to know the facts about everybody.

(MRS. WEBB, *a thin, serious, crisp little woman in the thirties, hurries downstairs L., tying on an apron (real), Xes to stove, shakes the grate, adds coal from a hod with a shovel, turns damper, etc.*)

There's Mrs. Webb comin' downstairs to get her breakfast too.

(DOC GIBBS, *a pleasant portly man in the thirties having started down L. on cue "facts about*

everybody," now appears up L. on Main Street,
yawning, carrying a bag in L. hand.)
(MRS. GIBBS *Xes to sink to pump water into coffee*
pot.)

That's Doc Gibbs. Got the call to go to Polish Town
at half past one this morning. (*Sound off R. of*
newspaper sliding along verandah.)

(JOE CROWELL, *a boy of eleven, starts down R.,*
Xing up onto Main St. and to C. Every few
feet he takes a newspaper from under his L.
arm and throws it upstage, whereat the sliding
sound is again heard.)

And here comes Joe Crowell deliverin' Mr. Webb's
Sentinel.

JOE. (*Turning into Main St.*) Mornin', Doc!
DR. GIBBS. Mornin', Joe!
JOE. Want your paper now?
DR. GIBBS. (*Setting bag on chair R. of up C.*)
Yes, I'll take it. (JOE *hands paper to* DR. GIBBS,
who unfolds it and stands by chair reading front
page.)

(MRS. GIBBS *Xes to put coffee pot on stove, then*
to cupboard to slice bacon.)

JOE. (*Xing rear to L. C.*) Anybody been sick,
Doc? (*Continues throwing papers.*)

(MRS. WEBB *Xes to cupboard to grind coffee into*
pot.)

DR. GIBBS. No. Some twins over in Polish Town
—Joe, I see your teacher Miss Foster is goin' to get
married.

JOE (*Xing back to chair L. of up C.*) Yes, sir, to a feller over in Concord.

DR. GIBBS. I declare. Well, how do you boys feel about that?

JOE. (*Seriously*) Well, of course it ain't none of my business—but I think if a person starts out to be a teacher she ought to stay one. (*Starts L. throwing papers.*)

(MRS. GIBBS *Xes to stove to put bacon in skillet.*)

DR. GIBBS. (*Smiling*) How's you knee, Joe?

JOE (*Stops up L.*) Fine, Doc, I never think about it at all. Only like you said, it always tell me when it's going to rain. (*Starts off to down L., throwing papers.*)

DR. GIBBS. What's it telling you today? Goin' to rain?

JOE. No sir.

DR. GIBBS. Sure?

(MRS. WEBB *puts coffee on stove.*)

JOE. Yes sir.

DR. GIBBS. Knee ever make a mistake?

JOE. No sir. (*Exits down L.*)

(DR. GIBBS *stands looking the newspaper over, yawns.*)

(MRS. GIBBS *Xes to cupboard, cuts several slices of bread, then cuts a pie.*)

(MRS. WEBB *mixes, rolls and cuts biscuits at table by stove.*)

STAGE MANAGER. I want to tell you something about that boy Joe Crowell there. Joe was awful bright—graduated from the High School here head of his class. So he got a scholarship to Boston

Techn—M.I.T., that is. Graduated head of his class from there too. It was all written up in the Boston papers at the time.

(DR. GIBBS *turns paper inside out, yawns.*)
(MRS. GIBBS *opens cupboard for tablecloth, Xes to spread it on table, Xes to cupboard for cup and spoon, Xes to set them for* DOC *at R. side of table.*)

Goin' to be a great engineer, Joe was, but the war broke out and he died in France. Yes sir, all that education for nothing. What business he had picking a quarrel with the Germans we can't make out to this day, but it all seemed perfectly clear to us at the time.

HOWIE NEWSOME. (*Off down L.*) Gid-ap, Bessie. What's the matter with you?

(MRS. GIBBS *Xes to stove, turns bacon, breaks four eggs into skillet.*)
(*The sound of MILK BOTTLES in a hand-rack is heard off L., and it continues through* HOWIE's *scene except when he sets down the rack.*)

STAGE MANAGER. Here comes Howie Newsome delivering the milk.

(HOWIE *starts from down L., an overalled country "character" of about thirty, carrying milkrack in L. hand; Xes up C., then down C. to trellis down L. He walks with a hitch.*)

HOWIE. Mornin', Doc!
DR. GIBBS. Mornin', Howie!
HOWIE. Somebody sick?

DR. GIBBS. Pair of twins over to Mrs. Goruslaw-ski's.

HOWIE. (*Starting down C. to trellis down L.*) Twins, eh? This town's gettin' bigger every year.

DR. GIBBS. (*Smiling*) Going to rain, Howie?

HOWIE. No, no. Fine day—it'll burn through. (*HORSE WHINNY effect off L.*) Come on, Bessie. (*Sets rack down, sets out two bottles in trellis.*)

DR. GIBBS. Hello, Bessie! (*Folding paper, putting it under L. arm, Xes to pat horse by chair L.. of C.*) How old is she, Howie?

HOWIE. (*Takes rack, Xes down R.*) Going on seventeen. Bessie's all mixed up about the route ever since the Lockharts stopped takin' their quart of milk every day. (MRS. GIBBS, *after glancing at* HOWIE *through window Xes into trellis.*) She wants to leave 'em a quart just the same—keeps scolding me the hull trip.

MRS. GIBBS. (*Opening door, which she leaves open.*) Good morning, Howie!

HOWIE. (*Sets rack down, hands her two bottles.*) Mornin', Mis' Gibbs. Doc's just comin' down the street.

MRS. GIBBS. Is he? Seems like you're late today.

(DR. GIBBS *takes bag, starts down C. to down L.*)

HOWIE. (*Taking rack, starts up C. and off R. without stopping*) Aya. Somep'n went wrong with the separator. Don't know what 'twas. (*Passing* DR. GIBBS.) Doc!

DR. GIBBS. Howie!

MRS. GIBBS. (*Taking milk to cupboard—calling upstairs*) Children! Children, time to get up!

HOWIE. Come on, Bessie!

MRS. GIBBS. George! Rebecca!

(MRS. WEBB *puts biscuits in oven, gets tablecloth, dishes, etc., from cupboard and lays table, making several trips.*)

(DR. GIBBS *enters house through trellis, sets bag down on steps.*)

MRS. GIBBS. (*Taking bread from cupboard to table.*) Everything all right, Frank?

DR. GIBBS. (*Laying newspaper on table*) Yes, I declare. Easy as kittens.

MRS. GIBBS. (*Xing to stove for coffee pot*) Bacon'll be ready in a minute. Set down and drink your coffee. (*Xing to pour coffee in his cup—then to set pot on stove.*) You can catch a couple hours sleep this mornin', can't you?

DR. GIBBS. (*Xing to sink, tosses hat off R., pumps water into basin, washes hands*) Mrs. Wentworth's comin' at eleven. Guess I know what it's about too. Her stomach ain't what it ought to be.

MRS. GIBBS. (*Xing to cupboard, picks out silver from drawer.*) All told, you won't get more'n three hours sleep. Frank Gibbs, I don't know what's goin' to become of you. I do wish you could go away some place and take a rest. I think it would do you good.

MRS. WEBB. (*Calling off L.*) Emily! Time to get up! Wally! Seven o'clock!

MRS. GIBBS. (*Xing to set three places at table, R. to L.*) I declare, you got to speak to George. Seems like somethin's come over him lately. He's no help to me at all. I can't even get him to cut me some wood.

DR. GIBBS. Is he sassy to you? (*Pulls down roller towel below sink, dries hands.*)

MRS. GIBBS. (*Xing to stove, picks up spatula*) No. He just whines! All he thinks about is that baseball— (*Xing R. a bit to call*) George! Rebecca! You'll be late for school.

DR. GIBBS. M-m-m.

MRS. GIBBS. George!

DR. GIBBS. George, look sharp!

GEORGE. Yes, Pa! (*Off R.*)

(MRS. GIBBS *turns eggs.*)

DR. GIBBS. Don't you hear your mother calling you? (*Xes to stairs.*)

MRS. WEBB. Walleee! You'll be late for school!

DR. GIBBS. Guess I'll go upstairs and take forty winks. (*Exit upstairs.*)

MRS. WEBB. Walleee! You wash yourself good or I'll come up and do it myself. (*Xes to table up R. to serve two dishes of oatmeal, which she places on table.*)

REBECCA. (*Off R.*) Ma! What dress shall I wear?

MRS. GIBBS. (*Xes to cupboard for two plates, Xes to stove.*) Don't make a noise. Your father's been out all night and needs his sleep. I washed and ironed the blue gingham for you special. (*Serves one plate and sets it on table for George.*)

REBECCA. Oh, Ma, I hate that dress.

MRS. GIBBS. Oh, hush-up-with-you!

REBECCA. Every day I go to school dressed like— like a sick turkey.

MRS. GIBBS. (*Serves second plate*) Now, Rebecca, you always look very nice.

REBECCA. (*Shrilly*) Mama, George's throwin' soap at me!

MRS. GIBBS. (*Xing to set plate for* REBECCA) I'll come up an' slap the both of you, that's what I'll do! (*Xes to cupboard for plate.*)

(*A FACTORY WHISTLE blows*)

STAGE MANAGER. (*Still by R. proscenium*) We got a mill in our town, too—hear it? (*Another*

WHISTLE.) Makes blankets. Cartwrights own it, and it's brung 'em a fortune.

(*Two beats after first whistle the* CHILDREN *have rushed downstairs,* GIRLS *leading. Entering R.,* REBECCA, 11, *and* GEORGE, *about 16, drop their strapped books on the steps and sit at table, he above, she L. of it. At once he starts eating sleepily, she to eat languidly, staring vaguely out.* EMILY *and* WALLY, *same ages, sit respectively above and R. of their table.* WALLY *hangs book bag on his chair back.* EMILY *puts her books carefully at her L.,* WALLY *opens a book and at once starts to read while both eat ravenously.*)
(MRS. GIBBS *sets plate on table. Xes to stove for coffee pot, Xes to pour it for* GEORGE, *replaces pot on stove, Xes to cupboard to pour glass of milk, Xes to place it for* REBECCA, *Xes to cupboard for butter.*)

MRS. WEBB. (*Xes to set down oatmeal for both children*) Children! Now I won't have it. Breakfast is just as good as any other meal and I won't have you gobblin' like wolves. It'll stunt your growth, that's a fact. Wally, put away your book!

WALLY. Oh, Ma! By ten o'clock I got to know all about Canada.

MRS. WEBB. (*Sits L. of table, eats*) You know the rule's well as I do—no books at table. As for me, I'd rather have my children healthy than bright.

(WALLY *puts book into bag, annoyed, then eats.*)

EMILY. I'm both, Mama, you know I am. I'm the brightest girl in school for my age. I have a wonderful memory.

MRS. WEBB. Eat your breakfast. (*Rises, Xes up*

R. for milk, returns to pour for both, replaces milk, returns to sit.)

MRS. GIBBS. (*Xing to R. of* GEORGE *to set down butter.*) I'll speak to your father about it when he's rested. Seems to me twenty-five cents a week's enough for a boy of your age. (*Xing to stove to pour own coffee*) I declare I don't know how you spend it all.

GEORGE. Aw, Ma,—I gotta lotta things to buy.

MRS. GIBBS. Strawberry phosphates—that's what you spend it on. (*Xes to between* CHILDREN *with cup, sips.*)

GEORGE. I don't see how Rebecca comes to have so much money. She has more'n a dollar.

REBECCA. (*Spoon in mouth, dreamily, to the audience*) I've been saving it up gradual.

MRS. GIBBS. Well, dear, I think it's a good thing to spend some every now an' then.

REBECCA. Mama, do you know what I love most in the world, do you? Money.

MRS. GIBBS. Eat your breakfast. (*Xes to set cup above stove.*)

(*An old-fashioned SCHOOLBELL is heard in the distance, off L.*)

REBECCA. (*Rising, running front of table to pick up her books*) There's the first bell. I gotta go.

(*All* CHILDREN *rise and rush for their books, then out to meet down C.* REBECCA *and* WALLY *lead out, followed by* GEORGE *and* EMILY. *On meeting, they ad lib greetings and, as they hurry up C. and off L. the* GIRLS *pair together, as do* GEORGE *and* WALLY, *chatting gaily.*)

(STAGE MANAGER *drifts off down R. as they pass up Main Street.*)

MRS. WEBB. (*As they start, following them into trellis*) Now walk fast, but you don't have to run. Wally pull up your pants at the knee. (*Clears table in two quick trips, putting dishes in sink, then gets two bowls from under sink.*)

MRS. GIBBS. (*As* CHILDREN *start, following them a few steps out of the trellis*) Tell Miss Foster I send her my best congratulations. Can you remember that?

REBBECA. Yes, Ma.

MRS. GIBBS. You look real nice, Rebecca. Pick up your feet! (*Goes in to cupboard, gets some cracked corn in her apron, and Xes through trellis to down R. C.*) (*Sounds of excited CHICKENS from off R.*)

MRS. GIBBS. (*Feeding chickens*) Here, chick-chick-chick— No, you go away, you— Here, chick-chick— What's the matter with you? Fight, fight, fight—that's all you do— You don't belong to me. Where'd you come from? (*Flings last of her feed, which causes loud clucks.*) (MRS. WEBB, *laden with two large bowls, Xes through trellis to sit L. end of bench, puts one bowl on floor, other on lap.*) Oh, don't be scared. Nobody's goin' to hurt you. (MRS. WEBB *strings beans into bowl on lap.*) (MRS. GIBBS *turning to catch sight of* MRS. WEBB, *hands on hip.*) Good morning, Myrtle. How's your cold?

MRS. WEBB. Well, I still get that tickling feeling in my throat. Told Charles I didn't know as I'd go to choir rehearsal tonight.

MRS. GIBBS. Have you tried singing over your voice?

MRS. WEBB. Yes, but somehow I can't do that and stay on the key. (MRS. GIBBS *Xes to sit R. of* MRS. WEBB.) While I am restin' myself I thought I'd string some of these beans.

MRS. GIBBS. Let me help you. Beans have been

good this year. (*Reaches for beans in bowl on ground.*)

MRS. WEBB. Aya, I decided to put up forty quarts if it kills me. Children say they hate 'em but I notice they're able to get 'em down all winter. (*Pause. CHICKEN NOISES.*)

MRS. GIBBS. (*After glance at chickens*) Now, Myrtle, I've got to tell you something, because if I don't tell somebody I'll burst.

MRS. WEBB. Why Julia Gibbs!

MRS. GIBBS. Myrtle, did one of those second-hand furniture men from Boston come to see you last Friday?

MRS. WEBB. (*Reaches for more beans*) No-o.

MRS. GIBBS. (*Reaches for more beans*) Well, he called on me. First I thought he was a patient wantin' to see Doctor Gibbs. (BOTH *stop work.*) 'N he wormed his way into my parlor, and, Myrtle Webb, he offered me three hundred and fifty dollars for Grandmother Wentworth's highboy, as I'm sitting here!

MRS. WEBB. Why, Julia Gibbs! (*Continues work.*)

MRS. GIBBS. (*Continues work*) He did! That old thing! Why, it was so big I didn't know where to put it and I almost give it to Cousin Hester Wilcox.

MRS. WEBB. Well, you're going to take it, aren't you?

MRS. GIBBS. I don't know.

MRS. WEBB. You don't know!—three hundred and fifty dollars? What's come over you?

MRS. GIBBS. Well, if I could get the Doctor to take the money and go away some place on a trip I'd sell it like that. (*Stops work.*) Y'know, Myrtle, it's been the dream of my life to see Paris, France. (*Glances slyly at* MRS. WEBB, *who is shocked, then laughs, hand to face.*) Oh, I don't know. It sounds

crazy, I suppose, but for years I been promising myself that if we ever had the chance—

MRS. WEBB. How's Doctor feel about it?

MRS. GIBBS. (*Continues work through scene*)
Well, I did beat about the bush a little and said that
if I got a legacy—that's the way I put it—I'd make
him take me.

MRS. WEBB. M-m-m— What did he say? (*Reaches
for beans.*)

MRS. GIBBS. You know how he is. I haven't heard
a serious word out of him, since I've known him.
No, he said, it might make him discontented with
Grover's Corners to go traipsin' about Europe; better let well enough alone, he says. Every two years
he makes a trip to the battlefields of the Civil War
and that's enough treat for anybody, he says.

MRS. WEBB. Well, Mr. Webb just *admires* the
way Doctor Gibbs knows everything about the Civil
War. Mr. Webb's a good mind to give up Napoleon
and move over to the Civil War, only Doctor Gibbs
being one of the greatest experts in the country just
makes him despair.

MRS. GIBBS. It's a fact, Doctor Gibbs is never so
happy as when he's at Antietam or Gettysburg. The
times I've walked over those hills, Myrtle, stopping
at every bush and pacing it all out, like we was going
to buy it.

MRS. WEBB. Well, if that second-hand man's
really serious about buyin' it, Julia, you sell it. And
then you'll get to see Paris, all right. Just keep drop-
pin' hints from time to time—that's how I got to
see the Atlantic Ocean, y'know.

MRS. GIBBS. Oh, I'm sorry I mentioned it. Only
it seems to me that once in your life before you die,
you ought to see a country where they don't talk in
English and don't even want to.

STAGE MANAGER. (*Entering briskly down R. Xes*

to R. C.) Thank you very much, ladies. (*To audience*) Now we'll skip a few hours.

(BOTH *women look up at him a moment in surprise, then* MRS. GIBBS *rises, brushing apron, and Xes through trellis R. and upstairs, nodding pleasantly at* STAGE MANAGER *as she passes him.* MRS. WEBB *picks up bowls and, after nod, rises to exit through trellis L. and behind tormentor, managing the bowls with difficulty.*)

But first we want a little more information about our town—kind of a scientific account you might say. So I've asked Professor Willard of our State University to sketch in a few details of our past history here. Professor Willard? (*The* STAGE MANAGER *peers off R.*)

(WILLARD, *a little dried-up man, flutters in nervously from down R., Xes to R. C. on apron.*)
(STAGE MANAGER *takes hat off.*)

May I introduce Professor Willard of our State University. Just a few brief notes, thank you, Professor—unfortunately our time is limited. (*Xes to lean against proscenium, puts hat on.*)

PROFESSOR WILLARD. Grover's Corners—mmm—let me see—Grover's Corners lies on the old pleiocene granite of the Appalachian range. I may say it's some of the oldest land in the world—we're very proud of that here. Of course there are some more recent outcroppings,—sandstone showing through a shelf of Devonian basalt, and some vestiges of Mezozoic shale, but these are comparatively new—perhaps two or three hundred million years. Some highly interesting fossils have been found—I may say, unique fossils—two miles north of the Peckham Farm—in Silas Peckham's cow-pasture. These may be seen in the museum at the University at any time—that is, at any reasonable time. (*Reaches for notes in inside pocket—to* STAGE MANAGER) Shall I read some of Professor Gruber's notes on the meteorological situation—mean precipitation, et cetera?

STAGE MANAGER. (*Xes R. C.*) Afraid we won't have time for that, Professor. We might have a few words on the history of man here—you know—

PROFESSOR WILLARD. Oh, anthropological data—

STAGE MANAGER. (*Smiling at him*) Er—yes.

PROFESSOR WILLARD. —Early Amerindian stock, Cotahatchee tribes—no evidence before the 10th Century of this era—now entirely disappeared— Oh, possible traces in three families—migration in early part of the 17th Century of English brachio-cephalic blue-eyed stock— Since then, some Slav and Mediterranean—

STAGE MANAGER. And the population, Professor Willard?

PROFESSOR WILLARD. Within the town limits: 2,640.

STAGE MANAGER. Just a moment Professor. (*He whispers into* PROFESSOR'S *ear*)

PROFESSOR WILLARD. Oh yes. The population at the moment is 2,642. The Postal District brings in 507 more—making a total of 3,149. Mortality, birth rates—constant. By McPherson's gauge: 6.032.

STAGE MANAGER. (*Urging him off down R.*) Thank you *very* much, Professor Willard. I know we're all very much obliged to you.

PROFESSOR WILLARD. Not at all, sir, not at all. (*Exits down R.*)

STAGE MANAGER. (*Xing R. C.*) Now the political and social report: Editor Webb— Oh, Mr. Webb?

MRS. WEBB. (*Appearing in trellis*) He'll be here in a minute— He just cut his hand whilst eatin' an apple. (*Exits*)

STAGE MANAGER. Thank you, Mrs. Webb. (*Turns R.*)

MRS. WEBB. (*Off R.*) Charles! Everybody's waitin'.

STAGE MANAGER. (*Xing R. to proscenium*) Mr. Webb is Publisher and Editor of *The Grover's Corners Sentinel*. That's our local paper, y'know.

MR. WEBB. (*Enters through trellis, Xing to L. C., real handkerchief about R. middle finger, finishing putting on his coat. A smiling, quizzical man in the late forties.*) Well,—I don't have to tell you that we're run here by a Board of Selectmen. All males vote at the age of 21. Women vote indirect. We're lower middle-class: sprinklin' of professional men—10% illiterate laborers. Politically, we're 86% Republicans; 6% Democrats; 4% Socialists; Rest, indifferent. Religiously, we're 85% Protestants; 12% Catholics; Rest, indifferent.

STAGE MANAGER. Have you any comments, Mr. Webb?

MR. WEBB. Very ordinary town, if you ask me. Little better behaved than most. Porbably a lot duller. But our young people here seem to like it well enough: 90% of 'em graduating from High School settle down right here to live—even when they've· been away to college.

STAGE MANAGER. Now, is there anyone in the audience who would like to ask Editor Webb any questions about our town?

WOMAN IN THE BALCONY. (*In high-pitched voice, in Balcony, L.*) Is there much drinking in Grover's Corners?

MR. WEBB. (*Amused, Xing few steps toward C.*) Well, ma'am, I wouldn't know what you'd call *much*. Sattidy nights the farmhands meet down in Ellery Greenough's stable and holler some. We've got one or two town drunks, but they're always having remorses every time an evangelist comes to town. No, ma'am, I'd say likker ain't a regular thing in the home here, except in the medicine chest. Right good for snake-bite, y'know—always was.

MAN AT BACK OF AUDITORIUM. (*At rear, L., in muffled tone*) Is there no one in town aware of—

STAGE MANAGER. Come forward, will you, where we can all hear you— What was it you wanted to ask?

MAN. (*Coming to under balcony front*) Is there no one in town aware of social injustice and industrial inequality?

MR. WEBB. Oh yes, everybody is,—somethin' terrible. Seems like they spend most of their time talking about who's rich and who's poor.

MAN. (*Forcefully*) Then why don't they do something about it?

MR. WEBB. (*Tolerantly*) Well, I dunno. I guess we're all huntin' like everybody else for a way the diligent and sensible can rise to the top and the lazy and quarrelsome sink to the bottom. But it ain't easy to find. Meantime, we do all we can to take care of those who can't help themselves and those that can we leave alone. Are there any other questions?

(MAN *retires up aisle.*)

ARTISTIC LADY IN A BOX. (*In Right Box—a Club Woman type*) Mr. Webb!

MR. WEBB. (*Xing L. of L. C.*) Yes, ma'am?

ARTISTIC LADY. Mr. Webb, is there any culture or love of beauty in—Grover's Corners?

MR. WEBB. (*Smiling*) Well, ma'am, there ain't much—not in the sense you mean. Come to think of it, there's some girls that play the piano over at High School Commencement; but they ain't happy about it. No, ma'am, there isn't much culture; but maybe this is the place to tell you that we've got a lot of pleasures of a kind here: we like the sun comin' up over the mountain in the morning, and we all notice a good deal about the *birds*. We pay a lot of attention to them. And we watch the change of the seasons: yes, everybody knows about them. But those other things—you're right, ma'am,—there ain't much—Robinson Crusoe and the Bible; and Handel's Largo, we all know that; and Whistler's Mother—those are just about as far as we go.

STAGE MANAGER. (*Xing C.*) Thank you, Mr. Webb.

(MR. WEBB *nods and exits through trellis L.*)

Now we'll go back to the town. It's two o'clock. All two thousand six hundred and forty-two have had their lunches, and all the dishes have been washed.

(MR. WEBB, *having removed his coat, starts pushing a lawn-mower, to appropriate sounds, from down L. above his house to L. of C. Turning, he retraces and makes another trip to L. of C.*)

The children have gone back to school—there's a buzzin' and a hummin' from the school buildings. Only a few buggies on Main Street, horses dozin' at the hitchin' posts. There's an early afternoon calm about the town. You all remember what it's like. (*Xing down R.*) Doc Gibbs is in his office, tappin' people and makin' 'em say "Ah". Mr. Webb's cuttin' his lawn over there,—one man in ten thinks it's a privilege to push his own lawn-mower.

(*Lights are now at high noon.*)
(*CHICKEN SOUNDS are again heard for a moment, then from off down L. a gay babble of young voices.*)

(MR. WEBB *kneels L. of C. to pick grass from edge of walk.*)

EMILY. (*Starts up from down L., walking sedately along Main Street. As she reaches the corner, she speaks off to her R.*) I can't, Lois. I've got to go home and help my mother. I promised. (*Starts to C.*)

MR. WEBB. Emily, walk simply. Who do you think you are today?

EMILY. (*Xing slowly up C. then to him*) Oh, Papa, you're terrible. One minute you tell me to stand up straight and the next minute you call me names. I just don't listen to you. (*Gives him an abrupt kiss on the back of the neck, then strolls to trellis down L., where she plays with roses.*)

MR. WEBB. (*Rising*) Golly, I never got a kiss from such a great lady before. (*Pushes lawn-mower off L.*)

GEORGE. (*Starting down L. on "You're terrible", has been throwing a ball high in the air and running forward to catch it—once up L., and now he rushes directly up C. and catches an unusually high one, bumping into someone. Facing up*) Excuse me, Mrs. Forrest.

STAGE MANAGER. (*Down R., imitating MRS. FORREST*) You go out and play in the fields, young man. You got no business playing baseball on Main Street.

GEORGE. (*Still facing up*) Awfully sorry, Mrs. Forrest. (*STAGE MANAGER smiles at audience and drifts off down R.*) (*GEORGE turns shyly down to chair R. of up C., peering around the WEBB house to see if EMILY is there*) Hello, Emily!

EMILY. (*Shyly, turning from trellis*) H'lo!

GEORGE. (*Edging to down C., socking L. mitt with baseball*) You made a fine speech in class.

EMILY. (*Facing out*) Well—I was really ready to make a speech about the Monroe Doctrine, but at the last minute Miss Corcoran made me talk about the Louisiana Purchase instead. I worked an awful long time on both of them.

GEORGE. (*Puts ball in back pocket, looks at own house, edges to R. of bench*) Gee, it's funny, Emily. From my window up there I can just see your head nights when you're doing your home-work over in your room. (BOTH *face mostly front, shy throughout*)

EMILY. (*Pleased at his admission*) Why, can you?

GEORGE. You certainly do stick to it, Emily. I don't see how you can sit still that long. I guess you must like school.

EMILY. Well, I always feel it's something you have to go through.

GEORGE. Yeah.

EMILY. I don't mind it really. It passes the time.

GEORGE. Yeah.—Emily, what do you think? We might work out a kinda telegraph from your window to mine; and once in a while you could give me a kinda hint or two about one of those Algebra problems. (EMILY *looks at him, shocked*) I don't mean the answers, Emily, of course not—just some little hint—

EMILY. Oh I think *hints* are allowed.—So-ah— If you get stuck, George, you whistle to me; and I'll give you some hints.

GEORGE. Emily, you're just naturally bright, I guess.

EMILY. (*Front*) I figure it's just the way a person's born.

GEORGE. Yeah. But, you see, I want to be a farmer, and my Uncle Luke says whenever I'm ready I can come over and work on his farm and if I'm any good I can just gradually have it.

EMILY. (*To him*) You mean the house and everything?

GEORGE. Yeah. (*Pause. Gets ball out, edges away up C.*) Well—I better be getting out to the baseball field. Thanks for the talk, Emily.—Good-afternoon, Mrs. Webb.

(EMILY, *wrapt in thoughts of* GEORGE, *looks after him*)

MRS. WEBB. (*Enter behind tormentor with bowls, Xes to sit on R. end of bench*) Good-afternoon, George!

GEORGE. So-long, Emily! (*Xing up R. then off down R., socking ball into L. hand.*)

EMILY. (*Casual, still in a dream*) So long, George!

MRS. WEBB. Emily, come and help me string these beans for the winter. (EMILY *sits L. of her and helps*) Well, George Gibbs let himself have a real conversation, didn't he? Why, he's growing up. How old would George be?

EMILY. (*Coming out of trance, protesting too much*) Oh, I don't know.

MRS. WEBB. Let's see. He must be almost sixteen.

EMILY. (*Changing the subject*) Mama, I made a speech in class today and I was very good.

MRS. WEBB. You must recite it to your father at supper. What was it about?

EMILY. The Lousiana Purchase. It was like silk off a spool. I'm going to make speeches all my life. —(*Holding up bean in both hands*) Mama, are these big enough?

MRS. WEBB. Try and get them a little bigger if you can.

EMILY. (*Thoughts on* GEORGE, *facing out*) Mama, will you answer me a question, serious?

MRS. WEBB. Seriously, dear—not serious.

EMILY. (*Annoyed*) Seriously,—will you?

MRS. WEBB. Of course, I will.

EMILY. (*After brief pause, expectantly*) Mama, am I good looking?

MRS. WEBB. (*Steals quick look at her*) Yes, of course you are. Both my children got good features. I'd be ashamed if they hadn't.

EMILY. (*Helplessly*) Oh, Mama, that's not what I mean. What I mean is:—am I *pretty?*

MRS. WEBB. I've already told you, yes. Now that's enough of that. You have a nice young pretty face. I never heard of such foolishness.

EMILY. Oh, Mama, you never tell us the truth about anything.

MRS. WEBB. I *am* telling you the truth.

EMILY. (*Wheedling a bit*) Mama, were *you* pretty?

MRS. WEBB. Yes, I was, if I do say it. I was the prettiest girl in town next to Mamie Cartwright.

EMILY. But Mama, you've *got* to say *something* about me. Am I pretty enough—to get anybody— to get people interested in me?

MRS. WEBB. (*Turning on her, firmly*) Emily, you make me tired! Now stop it! You're pretty enough for all *normal* purposes. (*Rises, taking bowl from bench*) Come along now and bring that bowl with you. (*Exits L. through trellis.*)

EMILY. (*Picking up bowl from floor and following*) Oh, Mama, you're no help at all.

(*During preceding scene the lights have gradually dimmed to late afternoon. Now they slowly change to night*)

STAGE MANAGER. (*Appears at proscenium R. with manuscript under arm. Xes C.*) Now, I think this is a good time to tell you that the Cartwright

interests have just begun building a new bank in
Grover's Corners—had to go to Vermont for the
marble, sorry to say. And they've asked a friend of
mine what they should put in the cornerstone for
people to dig up a thousand years from now. 'Course,
they've put in a copy of the *New York Times* and a
copy of Mr. Webb's *Sentinel*. We're kind of interested in this because some scientific fellas have found
a way of painting all that reading matter with a kind
of glue—sillicate glue—that'll make it keep a thousand—two thousand years— We're puttin' in a Bible
—'n a copy of the Constitution of the United States
'n a copy of William Shakespeare's *plays*. What do
you say, folks? What you you think? Y' know,
Babylon once had two million people in it, and
all we know about 'm is the names of the kings
and some copies of wheat contracts and—the sales
of slaves. Yes, every night all those families sat
down to supper, and the father came home from
his work, and the smoke went up the chimney,—
same as here. And even in Greece and Rome, all we
know about the real life of the people is what we
can piece together out of the joking poems and the
comedies they wrote for the theatre back then. So
I'm going to have a copy of this play (*Tapping the
manuscript*) put in the cornerstone so the people a
thousand years from now'll know a few simple facts
about us—more than the Treaty of Versailles and
the Lindbergh flight. See what I mean? So,—people
a thousand years from now,—this is the way we
were in the provinces North of New York at the
beginning of the Twentieth Century,—this is the
way we were—in our growing up and in our marrying, and in our living, and in our dying.

(*Choir, in orchestra pit, start "Blessed Be The Tie
That Binds". Rising on second phrase*)

Now we'll get back to Grover's Corners. It's evening.

(*Stepladders are moved on from R. and L. to R. C. and L. C. by* ASSISTANT STAGE MANAGERS. GEORGE *and* EMILY *enter R. and L. and mount ladders, where they do their arithmetic as if on windowsills*)
(STAGE MANAGER *Xes slowly down R.*)

You can hear the choir practice goin' on in the Congregational Church. The children are at home doin' their school work. The day is runnin' down like a tired clock. (*He listens a moment, then withdraws off down R.*)

(*At the end of the first line of the hymn, lights in the pit have come up showing the heads of the choir silhoutted as they face the stage, while* SIMON STIMSON *C. conducts them, facing the audience,—a long-faced "character" in his early thirties, now slightly drunk.*)

STIMSON. (*As verse ends*) All right, now do it again. And remember, ladies, music came into the world to give pleasure. Now try it again.

(EMILY *leans out window and peers at* GEORGE *a moment, then works again*)

(CHOIR *starts again "Blessed Be The Tie That Binds" with increasing volume. At the end of 2nd phrase:*)
(STIMSON *gently*)
Softer—
(*They still increase volume, and he suddenly becomes furious*)
Softer!
(CHOIR *stops*)

Now look here, everybody, get it out of your head
that music's only good when it's loud. You leave
loudness to the Methodists. You couldn't beat 'em,
even if you wanted to. Now again, tenors!
(CHOIR *sings three verses of "Blessed Be The Tie*
That Binds".)

GEORGE. Hsst, Emily!

EMILY. Hello!

GEORGE. Hello!

(*Pause*)

EMILY. I can't work at all. The moonlight's so
terrible.

GEORGE. (*Pause*) Emily, did you get the third
problem?

(DR. GIBBS *comes down stairs R. and sits R. of*
table, takes a book from it, reads)

EMILY. Which?

GEORGE. The *third*.

EMILY. Why, yes, George—that's the easiest of
them all.

GEORGE. I don't see it. Well, Emily, can you give
me a hint?

EMILY. I'll tell you *one thing:* the answer's in
yards.

(*First verse of hymn ends*)

GEORGE. ! ! ! in yards? How do you mean?

EMILY. In *square* yards.

GEORGE. Oh—in square yards.

EMILY. Yes, George, don't you see?

GEORGE. Yeah.

(*He does not see*)

EMILY. In square yards of *wall-paper.*

(*Faces out, having given more than a hint*)

GEORGE. (*A great light breaking*) Oh, I see.
Square yards of wall-paper! (EMILY *looks at him,*

beaming agreement. He erases and rewrites) Thanks
a lot, Emily.

EMILY. You're welcome. (*Looks out*) My, isn't
the moonlight *terrible?* (*Second verse of hymn
ends*) And choir practice going on. (*Listens hard a
moment, awed*) I think, if you hold your breath,
you can hear the train all the way to Contookuck!
(GEORGE *holds his breath, leaning out of window*)
Hear it?

GEORGE. M-m-m— What do you know!

EMILY. (*Reluctant*) Well, I guess I better go back
and try to work.

GEORGE. Goodnight, Emily.

EMILY. Goodnight, George. (BOTH *return un-
willingly to work, but almost immediately give up
and gaze at the moon, chins on hands*)

STIMSON. (*As third verse ends*) That's better;
but it ain't no miracle. (CHOIR *sits, at signal from
him*) 'Fore I forget it: How many of you'll be able
to come in Tuesday afternoon and sing at Fred
Hersey's wedding?—Show your hands. (CHOIR
raises hands above orchestra rail. DR. GIBBS *puts
down book, ponders*) That'll be fine. That'll be right
nice. Once again now: "Art thou weary, art thou
languid?" It's a question, ladies and gentlemen.
Make it talk.

DR. GIBBS. (*Calling off R. upstairs*) Oh, George,
can you come down a minute?

GEORGE. (*Listening upstage, as if stairs were behind him*) Yes, Pa. (*Descends ladder, stands above
table*)

STIMSON. And remember Sunday to take the second verse real soft and sort of die out at the end.
Ready? (*The* CHOIR *sings two verses of "Art thou
weary, art thou languid?", the lights fading on them
as they start.* STIMSON *disappears*)

DR. GIBBS (*Facing out throughout, gently
throughout*) Make yourself comfortable, George;

I'll only kep you a minute. (GEORGE *sits above table*) George, how old are you?

GEORGE. Me? I'm sixteen, almost seventeen.

DR. GIBBS. What do you want to do after school's over?

GEORGE. Why, you know, Pa, I want to be a farmer on Uncle Luke's farm.

DR. GIBBS. You'll be willing, will you, to get up early and milk and feed the stock—and you'll be able to hoe and hay all day?

GEORGE. Sure, I will. What do you mean, Pa?

DR. GIBBS. (*Never harshly*) Well, George, while I was in my office today I heard a funny sound—and what do you think it was? It was your mother chopping wood. (GEORGE *turns slowly L., ashamed*) There you see your mother—getting up early; cooking meals all day long; washing and ironing;—and still she has to go out in the backyard and chop wood. I suppose she just got tired of asking you. She just gave up and decided it was easier to do it herself. And you eat her meals, and put on the clothes she keeps nice for you, and you run off and play baseball,—like she's some hired girl we keep around the house but that we don't like very much. (GEORGE *snivels*) Well, I knew all I had to do was call your attention to it. Here's a handkerchief, son. (*Lays it on table,* GEORGE *takes it, blows nose*) George, I've decided to raise your spending money twenty-five cents a week. Not, of course, for chopping wood for your mother, because that's a sort of present you give her, but because you're getting older—and I imagine there are lots of things you must find to do with it.

GEORGE. Thanks, Pa.

DR. GIBBS. Let's see—tomorrow's pay day. You can count on it—- Hmm. (*Annoyed*) Probably Rebecca'll feel she ought to have some more too. (*Uneasy, to make conversation*) Wonder what could have happened to your mother. Choir practice never was as late as this before.

GEORGE. (*Still broken up*) It's only half-past eight, Pa.

DR. GIBBS. I don't know why she's in that old choir anyway. She hasn't got any more voice than an old crow! And traipsin' around the streets at this hour of the night! (*Finally, gently*) Just about time you retired, don't you think?

GEORGE. Yes, Pa. (*Lays handkerchief by father, who pockets it. GEORGE rises and mounts ladder, gazes at moon. DR. GIBBS soon resumes reading*)

MRS. SOAMES. (*Off L., linking arms with MRS. WEBB on her R., MRS. GIBBS on her L. She is in her thirties, the town gossip.*) Goodnight, Martha. Goodnight, Mr. Foster. (*WOMEN'S voices respond. The trio strolls up L. and stops to look back down L.*)

MRS. WEBB (*Calling off L.*) I'll tell Mr. Webb; I *know* he'll want to put it in the paper.

MRS. GIBBS. My, it's late!

MRS. SOAMES. Goodnight, Irma. (*They stroll silently to up C.*)

MRS. GIBBS. Real nice choir practice, wa'n't it?

MRS. WEBB. Um-m! (*They turn facing down up C.*)

MRS. GIBBS. Myrtle Webb! Look at that moon will you! Tsk—tsk—tsk! Potato weather, for sure. (*Pause*)

MRS. SOAMES (*Scandalized*) Well, naturally I didn't want to say a word about it in front of those others (*looks off rear L.*), but now we're alone—really, it's the worst scandal that ever was in this town!

MRS. GIBBS. What?

MRS. SOAMES. Simon Stimson!

(MRS. WEBB *turns half R., annoyed*)

MRS. GIBBS. Now, Louella!

MRS. SOAMES. But, Julia! To have the organist of a church, drink, and drunk year after year.

MRS. GIBBS. Louella!

MRS. SOAMES. Julia, you know he was drunk tonight.

MRS. GIBBS. (*Looking at moon*) Now Louella! We all know about Mr. Stimson, and we all know about the troubles he's been through, and Doctor Ferguson knows too, and if Doctor Ferguson keeps him on there in his job the only thing the rest of us can do is just not to notice it.

MRS. SOAMES. Not to notice it! But it's getting worse.

MRS. WEBB (*Acidly*) No, it isn't, Louella. It's getting better. I've been in that choir twice as long as you have. It doesn't happen anywhere near so often. My, I hate to go to bed on a night like this. Gracious, I'd better hurry. (*Gathers skirts at sides in both hands and rushes down through trellis and off L.*) Those children'll be sittin' up till all hours. Goodnight, Louella—Julia—(EMILY, *as* MRS. WEBB *passes her, excitedly blows out—i.e., switches off— the light that shines on her face from the ladder- shelf, and again gazes at the moon*)

MRS. GIBBS (*Xing down a few steps, turns to face* LOUELLA) Goodnight, Myrtle. Can you get home safe, Louella?

MRS. SOAMES. (*Xing L. a step*) Oh, it's as bright as day. I can see Mr. Soames scowling at the windows now. (*Laughs at the thoughts*) You'd think we'd been to a dance the way the men folk carry on! (BOTH *laugh and start on their ways*) Goodnight, Julia.

MRS. GIBBS. Goodnight, Louella.

MRS. SOAMES. See you on Sunday.

MRS. GIBBS. See you then. (MRS. SOAMES *exits slowly off R.* MRS. GIBBS *sweeps through trellis to above L. end of table, takes her hat off, jabs it with hatpin, lays it on table*) (GEORGE *snaps off the light on his ladder-shelf as his mother goes by*) Well, we had a real good time.

DR. GIBBS. (*Looks at pocket watch*) You're late enough.

MRS. GIBBS. Why, Frank, it ain't any later 'n usual.

DR. GIBBS. And you stopping at the corner to gossip with a lot of hens.

MRS. GIBBS. Now, Frank, don't be grouchy. (*Xing to take his R. arm*) Come out and smell my heliotrope in the moonlight. Come on! Uh! (*He puts book reluctantly on table, rises, and they stroll, her arm in his, out trellis to C. A BOBWHITE calls three times. They speak quietly*)

MRS. GIBBS. (*Sighing*) Isn't that wonderful? (*They stop C. surveying the moonlit scene out front*) What did you do all the time I was away?

DR. GIBBS. (*Interested, though he tries to disapprove*) Oh, I read—as usual— What were the girls gossiping about tonight?

MRS. GIBBS. Well, believe me, Frank—there's something to gossip about.

DR. GIBBS. Hmm! Simon Stimson far gone, was he?

MRS. GIBBS. Worst I've ever seen 'him. How'll that end, Frank? Doctor Ferguson can't forgive him forever.

DR. GIBBS. I guess I know more about Simon Stimson's affairs than anybody in this town. Some people ain't made for small town life. (*She takes arm from his, turns to gaze half R.*) I don't know how that'll end; but there's nothing we can do but just leave it alone—(*Pause*) Get in.

MRS. GIBBS. (*Taking his arm again*) No, not yet. —Frank, I'm worried about you.

DR. GIBBS. (*Smiling*) What are you worried about?

MRS. GIBBS. I think it's my duty to make plans for you to get a real rest and change. (DR. GIBBS *laughs, breaks, crosses to her R.*) And if I get that legacy, I'm going to insist on it.

DR. GIBBS. Now, Julia, there's no sense in going over that again.

MRS. GIBBS. Frank, you're just *unreasonable!*

DR. GIBBS. (*Pats her back, pushes her ahead pouting, into house*) Come on, Julia, it's gettin' late. First thing you know you'll catch cold— I gave George a piece of my mind tonight. (*Turns inside trellis to close door*) (MRS. GIBBS *picks up string from floor and, winding it up, goes to cupboard to leave it*) I reckon you'll have your wood chopped,— for awhile anyway. No, no. Start gettin' upstairs. (*Goes to table, holds hand out as if to blow out lamp, stops to listen*)

MRS. GIBBS. Oh dear, there's always so many things to pick up, seems like. (*Xing to table for hat*) You know, Frank, Mrs. Fairchild always locks her front door every night. (DR. GIBBS *blows out lamp*) (MRS. GIBBS *starts upstairs and off R.*) All those people up that part of town do.

DR. GIBBS. (*Following her*) They're all gettin' citified, that's the trouble with them. They haven't got anythin' fit to burgle and everybody knows it.

(*There is the sound of CRICKETS as* REBECCA, *starting down R. as* MRS. GIBBS *starts up steps, tiptoes to* GEORGE'S *ladder and climbs up beside him, to his L.*)

GEORGE. (*As she is half-way up*) Get out, Rebecca. There's only room for one at this window.

REBECCA. (*At the moon*) Well, let me look just a minute.

GEORGE. Use you own window.

REBECCA. I did; but there's no moon there—George, do you know what I think, do you? I think maybe the moon's getting nearer and nearer and there'll be a big 'splosion.

GEORGE. Rebecca, you don't know anything. If the moon were getting nearer, the men that sit up all night with telescopes would see it first and they'd tell us about it, and it'd be in all the newspapers. (*Pause*)

REBECCA. George, is the moon shining on South America, Canada and half the whole world?

GEORGE. Well—prob'ly is.

(CONSTABLE WARREN, *an old man, starting off R. on "Telescopes," Xes up Main Street to C., trying a doorknob every few feet*)

(MR. WEBB *starts from down L., hands in hip pockets, Xes to up C.*)

STAGE MANAGER. (*Appears at proscenium down R.*) Nine-thirty. Most of the lights in town are out. There's Constable Warren trying a few doors on Main Street. And here comes Editor Webb, after putting his newspaper to bed. (*Exits down R.*)

MR. WEBB. (*As he turns corner*) Good evening, Bill.

CONSTABLE WARREN. (*Up C.*) Evenin', Mr. Webb.

MR. WEBB. Quite a moon!

CONSTABLE WARREN. (*Looks at it, unmoved*) Yeh! (*They stop up C. to chat*)

MR. WEBB. All quiet tonight?

(STIMSON *starts down L., trying hard to walk soberly, head held high*)

CONSTABLE WARREN. Simon Stimson is rollin' around a little. Just saw his wife movin' out to hunt for him so I looked the other way—there he is now.

MR. WEBB. (*As* STIMSON *turns corner*) Good evening, Simon. Town seems to have settled down for the night pretty well. (*Pause, while* STIMSON *comes up to him quite close and stops*) Good evening. Yes, most of the town's settled down for the night, Simon. I guess we better do the same. Can I walk along a ways with you? (STIMSON *stares a moment, then staggers above them, stops R. of* CONSTABLE *a moment, lifts his head in pleading agony, and exits R. slowly and unsteadily.* MEN *turn to watch as he starts off*) (*As he nears R. corner*) Good night.

CONSTABLE WARREN. I don't know how that's goin' to end, Mr. Webb.

MR. WEBB. Well, he's seen a peck of trouble, one thing after another. Oh, Bill—if you see my boy smoking cigarettes, just give him a word, will you? He thinks a lot of you, Bill.

CONSTABLE WARREN. I don't think he smokes no cigarettes, Mr. Webb, Leastways, not more'n two or three a year.

MR. WEBB. Hm. I hope not. (*Starts down C.*) Good night, Bill.

CONSTABLE WARREN. Good night, Mr. Webb. (*Exits L. trying doors*)

MR. WEBB. (*Stops R. of ladder, sensing someone in window*) Who's that up there? Is that you Myrtle?

EMILY. (*Pooh-poohing him*) No, it's me, Papa.

MR. WEBB. (*Xing down two steps*) Why aren't you in bed?

EMILY. I don't know. I just can't sleep yet, Papa. The moonlight's so *won*-derful. And the smell of Mrs. Gibbs's heliotropes. Can you smell it?

MR. WEBB. (*Turns to smell, turns back*) Hm—

Yes. Haven't any troubles on your mind, have you, Emily?

EMILY. *Troubles,* Papa. *No.*

MR. WEBB. Well, don't let you mother catch you. (*Starts to down L.*) Good night, Emily.

EMILY. Good night, Papa. (MR. WEBB *exits through trellis, whistling "Blessed Be The Tie That Binds"*)

REBECCA. (*When he is off, looking at moon throughout*) I never told you about that letter Jane Crofut got from her minister when she was sick. He wrote Jane a letter and on the envelope the address was like this: It said: "Jane Crofut; The Crofut Farm, Grover's Corners; Sutton County; New Hampshire; United States of America."

GEORGE. What's funny about that?

REBECCA. (*Momentarily at him, with increasing awe*) But listen, it's not finished: the United States of America; Continent of North America; Western Hemisphere; the Earth; the Solar System; the Universe; the Mind of God,—that's what it said on the envelope.

GEORGE. What do you know!

REBECCA. Yep, and the postman brought it just the same.

GEORGE. What do you know! (Pause. *CRICK-ETS*)

STAGE MANAGER. (*Appearing down R.*) That's the end of the First Act, friends. You can go out and smoke now, those that smoke.

(*The stage lights dim and the pilot light fades in. The* ACTORS *walk off during the dim*)

END OF ACT ONE

ACT TWO

In the intermission, five minutes after the close of Act I, the STAGE MANAGER, *hat on and pipe in mouth, strolls on and pushes both ladders off; also sets chair L. of table L. C. half toward audience, for Mr. Webb's later use, and pushes chair L. of table R. C. close under table, then strolls off.*

A minute before "curtain time" the stage lights fade gradually into an early-morning blue. The pin-spot on the R. proscenium then fades in and the STAGE MANAGER *enters to lean against proscenium, watching late smokers. As he waits the house and pilot light fades out. When fade is complete, he crosses to C., where another pin-spot picks him up as the R. one fades.*
During the opening speech morning light is gradually established.

STAGE MANAGER. Three years have gone by. The sun's come up over a thousand times. Summers and winters have cracked the mountains a little bit more and the rains have brought down some of the dirt. Some babies that weren't even born before, have begun talkin' regular sentences already; and a number of people who thought they were right young and spry have noticed that they can't bound up a flight of stairs like they use-ta, without their hearts flutterin' a little. All that can happen in a thousand days. Nature's been pushin' and contrivin' in other ways, too—a number of young people fell in love and got married. Yes, the mountain got bit away a few fractions of an inch; millions of gallons of water have passed by the mill; and here and there a new home was set up under a roof. Almost everybody in the world gets married,—you know what I mean? In our town there aren't hardly any exceptions. Most everybody climbs into their grave married. The First Act was called The Daily Life; this Act is called Love and Marriage. So: It's three years later. It's 1904. It's July 7th, just after High School Commencement. That's the time most of our young people jump up and get married. Soon as they've passed their last examinations in Solid Geometry and Cicero's Orations, looks like they suddenly feel themselves fit to get married— It's early morning again. (*Distant THUNDER effect*) Only this time it's been raining. It's been pouring and thundering. Mrs. Gibbs's garden—and Mrs. Webb's here—drenched. All those bean-poles and pea-vines,—drenched. All yesterday, over there on Main Street the rain looked like curtains being blown along. (*More THUNDER. He looks up and out*) Hm—don't know now—may begin again any minute. (*DISTANT TRAIN WHISTLE. He looks at pocket watch*) There's the 5:10 train for Boston.

(Mrs. Gibbs *and* Mrs. Webb *enter by their respective stairs.* Mrs. Gibbs *again raises shade and window and makes her wood fire.* Mrs. Webb *shakes the grate, adds coal to her stove, turns damper, fills coffee pot at sink*)

And there's Mrs. Gibbs and Mrs. Webb come down to make breakfast, just as if this were an ordinary day. (*Turning a few steps up*) I don't have to point out to the women in the audience that both these ladies they see before them, both these ladies cooked three meals a day, one of 'em for twenty years and the other for forty—and no summer vacation.

(MRS. WEBB *Xes with pot to cupboard and grinds coffee*)

They raised two children apiece, washed, cleaned the house, and never had a nervous breakdown.

(MRS. GIBBS. *grinds coffee into pot above stove.* MRS. WEBB *Xes to put pot on stove, starts to make corn bread*)

Never thought themselves hard-used, either —It's like what one of those Middle West poets said: You got to love life to have life, and you got to have life to love life— It's what they call a vicious circle.

HOWIE. (*Off down L.*) Gid-ap, Bessie! (*Sound of MILK BOTTLES in rack starts off L. and continues through scene as in Act I. MRS. GIBBS Xes to sink to pump water into pot*)

STAGE MANAGER. (*Xing down R.*) And there comes Howie Newsome and Bessie, deliverin' the milk.

(*Sound of newspapers slapping on verandahs off R. HOWIE starts down L., Xes to up C., rack in L. hand*)

And there's Si Crowell deliverin' the papers like his brother before him. (*Watches a moment from proscenium, then drifts off down R.*)

(MRS. GIBBS *Xes to pump water into coffee into coffee pot.*)

(SI CROWELL, 11, *enters-down R. following route up C. throwing newspapers, per Joe Crowell's routine in Act I.*)

SI. Mornin', Howie.

HOWIE. Mornin', Si. Anythin' in the papers I ought to know. (*Stops up C. by chair L. of C., sits on its back, sets rack down*)

(MRS. GIBBS *puts coffee on stove, Xes to cupboard and prepares two pieces of French toast. She holds back tears for a moment. MRS. WEBB Xes to cupboard to slice bacon and rearrange the shelves*)

SI. (*Stops by chair R. of C.*) Nothin' much, except we're losin' about the best baseball pitcher Grover's Corners ever had.

HOWIE. Aya, reckon he is.

SI. And now all he'll be doin' is pitchin' hay.

(*HORSE WHINNY off L.*)

HOWIE. (*Looking off L.*) Whoa, Bessie! Guess I can stop and talk if I've a-mind to!

SI. He could hit, too. And run bases.

HOWIE. Aya. Mighty fine ballplayer.

SI. I don't see how he could give up a thing like that just to get married. Would you have, Howie?

HOWIE. Can't tell, Si. Never had no talent that way. (CONSTABLE WARREN *starts down L., Xes up L. to up C. He walks with a cane. A little older than before*)

CONSTABLE WARREN. Mornin', Howie.

HOWIE. Hello, Bill. You're up early. (MRS. GIBBS *puts French toast into skillet on stove, then gets cloth from cupboard, lays table, sets cup and spoon for dog*)

SI. Mornin', Mr. Warren.

CONSTABLE WARREN. Seein' if there's anything I can do to prevent a flood. River's been risin' all night. (*He stops between the two*)

HOWIE. Si Crowell here's all broke up about George Gibbs' retiring from baseball.

CONSTABLE WARREN. Yes, sir, that's the way it goes. In '84 we had a player, Si, even George Gibbs couldn't a touched him. Name a Hank Todd. Went

down to Maine and become a parson. Wonderful
ballplayer. (*Xes rear* SI *and off R., looking up C.
at sky*) Howie, how's the weather seem to you?

(SI *starts off L., throwing newspapers, exits*)

HOWIE. (*Picking up rack, Xing down R.*) Oh,
'tain't bad. Think mebbe it'll clear up for good.
(MRS. WEBB *puts bacon on stove, then washes and
dries hand at sink*) (MRS. GIBBS *Xes down to open
door and meet* HOWIE)

HOWIE. Bill!

CONSTABLE WARREN. Howie!

HOWIE. Morning, Mrs. Gibbs. (*Sets rack down*)

MRS. GIBBS. Good morning, Howie.

HOWIE. Too bad about the weather. It's been
raining so heavy that maybe it'll clear up.

MRS. GIBBS. Certainly hope it will.

HOWIE. How much did you want today?

MRS. GIBBS. I'm going to have a houseful of re-
lations, Howie. Looks to me like I'll need three-a-
milk and two-a-cream.

HOWIE. (*Handing her two bottles, setting three
on doorstep*) Three a milk and two a cream. My
wife says to tell you we hope they'll be happy,—
know they will. (*Picks up rack, starts to down L.*)

MRS. GIBBS. (*Calling after him*) Thanks a lot,
Howie. Tell your wife I hope she gets to the wedding. (MRS. WEBB *Xes down to trellis*) (MRS.
GIBBS *takes two bottles to cupboard, returns for
other three, then Xes to turn french toast, winking
back tears*)

HOWIE. Maybe she kin. She'll get there if she kin.
Good morning, M's Webb. (*Sets rack down.*)

MRS. WEBB. Oh, good morning, Mr. Newsome.
I told you four quarts of milk, but I hope you can
spare me another.

HOWIE. (*Kneeling, hands her two bottles, sets four on doorstep*) Yes'm—and two-a-cream.

MRS. WEBB. (*Looking up.*) Will it start raining again, Howie?

HOWIE. (*Looking up*) Well— I was just sayin' to M's Gibbs as how it may clear off. (*Rises, takes rack, starts up C. and off R.*) Mrs. Newsome told me special to tell you as how we hope they'll be happy, M's Webb,—know they will.

MRS. WEBB. (*Calling after him*) Thank you, and thank Mrs. Newsome; and we're counting on seeing you at the church.

HOWIE. Yes, M's Webb. We hope to git there all right. Couldn't miss that. Come on, Bessie! (*MRS. WEBB takes two bottles to table above stove, returns for four more. MRS. GIBBS near stove stops to blow nose, on verge of tears*)

DR. GIBBS. (*Enters downstairs R. to R. of table. Trying to be cheerful*) Well, Ma, the day has come. You're losing one of your chicks.

MRS. GIBBS. (*Covering up tears*) Frank Gibbs, don't you say another word. I feel like cryin' every minute. (*Xes to pour coffee at table for him*) Sit down and drink your coffee. (*MRS. WEBB peels and slices potatoes at table above stove.*)

DR. GIBBS. (*Sits R. of table, tucks napkin into neck, puts sugar in coffee*) The groom's up shaving himself, only there ain't an awful lot to shave— (*MRS. GIBBS sets pot on stove and Xes to cupboard for silver*) whistling and singing like he's glad to leave us.— Every now and then he says "I do" to the mirror, but it don't sound convincing to *me*. (*Blows coffee and drinks*)

MRS. GIBBS. (*Xing to table to set places for self and REBECCA*) I declare, Frank, I don't know how he'll get along. I've arranged his clothes, and seen to it his feet are dry and he's got warm things on—

they're too young, Frank. Emily won't think of such things. He'll catch his death-a-cold within a week.

DR. GIBBS. I remember my wedding morning, Julia.

MRS. GIBBS. (*Xing to stove to turn french toast*) Now don't start that, Frank Gibbs.

DR. GIBBS. (*Smiling*) I was the scaredest young fella in the state of New Hampshire. I thought I'd made a mistake for sure. (MRS. GIBBS *Xes to cupboard to pour milk*) When I saw you coming down that aisle I thought you were the prettiest girl I'd ever seen; but the only trouble was that I'd never seen you before. There I was in the Congregational Church marryin' a total stranger! (MRS. WEBB *puts potatoes on stage to German-fry. Then sets table from cupboard in three trips.*)

MRS. GIBBS. (*Xing to table with milk for RE-BECCA*) And how do you think *I* felt? (*Xing to above to serve his toast*) Frank, weddings are perfectly awful things. Farces,—that's what they are! (*Xing to table to set plate before him*) Here, I've made something for you.

DR. GIBBS. Why, Julia Hersey! French toast!

MRS. GIBBS. (*Pleased*) 'Tain't hard to make and I had to do *something*. (*Turns suddenly serious and Xes to stove, serves self.*)

DR. GIBBS. (*Pause. DR. GIBBS pours syrup round and round four times, then:*) How'd you sleep last night, Julia? (*Eats*)

MRS. GIBBS. (*Xing to sit above table with own plate and coffee*) Well, I heard a lot of the hours struck off. (*Takes sugar and cream*)

DR. GIBBS. (*Thoughtfully, facing half out*) Aya, I get a shock every time I think of George setting out to be a family man—that great gangling thing! I tell you, Julia, there's nothing so terrifying in the world as a son. The relation of father and son is the damndest, awkwardest—

Mrs. Gibbs. (*Stirs coffee*) Well, mother and daughter's no picnic, let me tell you— (*Drinks*)

Dr. Gibbs. They'll have a lot of troubles, I suppose, but that's none of our business. Everybody has a right to their own troubles. (Mrs. Webb *faces up, washes dishes*)

Mrs. Gibbs. (*Drinking coffee, reminiscent*) Aya —people are meant to live two-by-two in this world. 'Tain't natural to be lonesome. (*Cuts toast*)

Dr. Gibbs. (*After a slight pause; laughing*) Julia, do you know one of the things I was scared of when I married you?

Mrs. Gibbs. Oh, go along with you! (*Eats*)

Dr. Gibbs. I was afraid we didn't have material for conversation more'n'd last us a few weeks. (Both *laugh heartily*) I was afraid we'd run out and eat our meals in silence, that's a fact. Well, you and I been conversing for twenty years now without any noticeable barren spells. (*Eats*) (Mrs. Webb *dries hands on towel, starts to weep.*)

Mrs. Gibbs. Well, good weather, bad weather, 'tain't very choice, but I always find something to say. Did you hear Rebecca stirrin' around upstairs? (*Rises, taking both plates. Xes to sink to scrape plates*) (Mrs. Webb *Xes to sit above table, facing L., covers apron*)

Dr. Gibbs. No. Only day of the year Rebecca hasn't been managing everybody's business up there. She's hiding in her room. I got the idea she's crying.

Mrs. Gibbs. (*Xing two steps R.*) Lord's sakes— this has got to stop. Rebecca! Rebecca! Come and get your breakfast.

(Dr. Gibbs *wipes mouth with napkin*)

George. (*Runs down stairs R. Cheerily, Xing to slap Father's back*) Good morning, everybody.

Only four more hours to live! (*Gestures cutting throat with "K-k-k-z-t" sound. Xes into trellis down R.* GIBBS *looks annoyed at sound.*)

MRS. GIBBS. (*Xing to half to table*) George Gibbs, where are you going?

GEORGE. (*Stepping back into room*) Just stepping across the grass to see my girl. (DR. GIBBS *folds napkin*)

MRS. GIBBS. Now, George, you put on your rubbers. It's raining torrents. You don't go out of this house without you're prepared for it. (DR. GIBBS *rises, Xes to stairs, stops*)

GEORGE. Aw, Ma—it's just a *step*.

MRS. GIBBS. George. (*Takes dog's plate and cup to sink, scrapes plate*) You'll catch your death-a-cold and cough all through the service. (GEORGE *starts doggedly out trellis*)

DR. GIBBS. George, do as your mother tells you! (*Exits upstairs*) (GEORGE *droops, Xes to sit on steps, puts on rubbers*)

MRS. GIBBS. (*To cupboard for cup, sets it on table*) From tomorrow on you can kill yourself in all weathers, but while you're in my house you'll live wisely, thank you. (*Xing to stove for pot, starts to table with it*) Perhaps Mrs. Webb isn't used to callers at seven in the morning. (GEORGE *rises, Xes into trellis*) Here, take a cup of coffee first!

GEORGE. (*Gaily*) 'Be back in a minute. (*Runs, jumping puddles to down L. and through trellis*)

(MRS. GIBBS *shakes head in annoyance, takes cup, pours coffee back in pot on stove, exits upstairs.*)

GEORGE. (*Xing in above to R. of her, cheerily*) Good morning, Mother Webb.

MRS. WEBB. Good morning, George. Goodness!

You frightened me! (*Rises, turns to him*) Now, George—I hate to say it—you can stand here a minute out of the rain—but really—you understand, George, I can't ask you in.

GEORGE. Why not—?

MRS. WEBB. Why, George, you know's well as I do—the groom can't see his bride on his wedding day, not until he sees her in church.

(MR. WEBB *starts downstairs*)

GEORGE. Aw,—that's just a superstition. Good morning, Mr. Webb.

MRS. WEBB. Good morning, George. (*Xes to stove for coffee pot, takes it to up L. of table*)

GEORGE. (*Laughing*) Mr. Webb, you don't believe in that superstition, do you?

MR. WEBB. There's a lot of common-sense in superstitions, George. (*Sits L. of table*)

MRS. WEBB. (*Pouring coffee for him*) Millions have folla'd it, George, and don't you be the first to fly in the face of custom. (*Xes to replace pot on stove*)

(MR. WEBB *takes four spoons of sugar*)

GEORGE. How is Emily?

MRS. WEBB. She hasn't waked up yet. I haven't heard a sound out of her. (*Pouring coffee at stove*)

GEORGE. Emily's asleep!!

MRS. WEBB. No wonder! We were up til' all hours sewing and packing. (*Sets cup for* GEORGE) Now, I'll tell you what I'll do, George; you set down here a minute with Mr. Webb and drink this cup of coffee; (*Xing to stairs*) and I'll run upstairs and see she don't come down and surprise you. There's some bacon, too. (*Going upstairs*) But don't be long about it.

(*Long pause.* GEORGE *sits above table, uses sugar, stirs, steals look at* MR. WEBB. WEBB, *facing half out, embarrassed, dunks doughnut and eats ravenously*)

MR. WEBB. Well, George, how are you?

GEORGE. (*About to drink, sets cup down*) I'm fine. (*Pause. Earnestly*) Mr. Webb, what common-sense *could* there be in a superstition like that?

MR. WEBB. (*Still half out*) Well, George—on the wedding morning a girl's head's full of—oh, you know—clothes and—one thing and another. Don't you think that's probably it? (*Dunks and eats*)

GEORGE. I—uh—yes. I never thought of that.

MR. WEBB. A girl's apt to be a mite nervous on her wedding day.

GEORGE. (*Stirring coffee*) Gee, I wish a person could get married without all that marching up and down.

MR. WEBB. Every man that's ever lived has felt that way, George, but it hasn't been any use. It's the women-folk who've built up weddings, my boy. For a while now the women have it all their own. (*Drinks from saucer*) A man looks pretty small at a wedding, George. All those good women standing shoulder to shoulder, making sure that the knot's tied in a mighty public way. (*Cuts food and eats*)

GEORGE. (*Earnestly*) Well, *you* believe in it, don't you, Mr. Webb?

MR. WEBB. (*Quietly*) Yes. (*With alacrity, suddenly looking at* GEORGE) Oh, yes! Now, don't misunderstand me, George. Marriage is a wonderful thing. A wonderful thing. Don't you forget that, George.

GEORGE. No, sir. (*Pause*) Mr. Webb, how old were you when you got married?

MR. WEBB. Well, you see—I'd been to college

and I'd taken a little time to get settled. But Mrs.
Webb, she wasn't much older than what Emily is.
(*Stirring coffee*) Oh, age hasn't got much to do with
it, George, compared with—other things. (*Drinks*)

GEORGE. What were you going to say, Mr. Webb?

MR. WEBB. I don't know. Was I going to say
something? (GEORGE *is confused*) (*Pause*) (MR.
WEBB *sits back, crosses knees, folds arms*—) George,
I was remembering the other night the advice my
father gave me when I got married. Yes, he said:
"Charles," he said: "start right off showin' who's
boss. Best thing to do is to give an order about
something, even if it don't make sense, just so she'll
learn to obey," he said. (GEORGE *is more perplexed,
looks out throughout*) Then he said: "If anything
about her irritates you, her conversation or anything, get right up and leave the house; that'll make
it clear to her." And, oh, yes, he said: "Never let
your wife know about how much money you have,
never."

GEORGE. (*Frightened and flabbergasted*) Well, I
couldn't exactly—

MR. WEBB. So I took the opposite of his advice
and I've been happy ever since. (GEORGE *rests chin
on L. hand, completely puzzled.* MR. WEBB *smiles
at his confusion. He has obviously invented the
story*) So let that be a lesson to you never to ask
advice of anybody on personal matters (*Faces him*)
George, are you going to raise chickens on your
farm?

GEORGE. What?

MR. WEBB. Are you raising chickens on your
farm?

GEORGE. (*Hitches chair a bit nearer, enthusiastic*)
Yes, Uncle Luke has never gone in for chickens
much—but I been figuring on readin' up—

MR. WEBB. George, a book came into my office
on the Philo System of raising chickens. I wish

you'd read it. I'm thinking of beginning in a small way myself, in the back yard! I'm going to put an incubator in the cellar—

MRS. WEBB. (*Enters downstairs. Xes to above* MR. WEBB) Charles Webb, are you talking about that incubator again? I thought you two'd be talking about things worth while!

MR. WEBB. (*Firm and sarcastic*) Well, Myrtle, if you want to give the boy some good advice, I'll go upstairs.

MRS. WEBB. (*Pulls* GEORGE *up and forces him out through trellis*) George, Emily's got to come down and eat her breakfast! She sends you her love, but she doesn't want to lay her eyes on you. Goodbye.

GEORGE. (*More perplexed than ever*) Goodbye. (GEORGE *Xes slowly home, avoiding a puddle C., and upstairs,* MRS. WEBB *stands above trellis watching*)

MR. WEBB. (*Rise*) Myrtle, guess you didn't know about that older superstition.

MRS. WEBB. What do you mean, Charles?

MR. WEBB. (*Wagging his finger*) Since the caveman. No bridegroom should see his father-in-law on the day of the wedding, or near it. (*Exit upstairs*) Now remember that. (MRS. WEBB, *eyes following him in surprise, exits behind tormentor*)

STAGE MANAGER. (*Entering down R., Xing to C.*) Thank you very much, Mr. and Mrs. Webb. Now I have to interrupt again here. You see, we want to know how all this began,—this wedding, this plan to spend a life-time together. I'm awfully interested in how big things like that begin. You know how it is: you're twenty-one or twenty-two any you make some decisions; then whisssh! you're seventy; you've been a lawyer for fifty years, and that white-haired lady by your side has eaten over fifty thousand meals with you. How do such things

begin? George and Emily are going to show you
now the conversation they had when they first knew
that—as the saying goes—they were meant for one
another. But before they do that I want you to try
and remember what it was like when you were very
young, and particularly the days when you were first
in love; when you were like a person sleep-walking,
and you didn't quite see the street you were walking
in, and you didn't quite hear everything that was
said to you. You're just a little bit crazy. Will you
remember that, please? Now they'll be coming out
of High School at three o'clock. George has just
been elected President of the Senior Class and as
this is June, that means he'll be President of the
Senior Class all next year. And Emily's just been
elected Secretary and Treasurer. (*Young voices are
heard off L. He starts R.*) Aya, there they are coming down Main Street now. (*Voices mount gaily,
as* STAGE MANAGER *picks up board behind R. tormentor, Xes rear of table to place it across chair-
backs left of table R. C., to serve as a soda-fountain,
then brings on two stools to place behind board.
Exits down R.*)

EMILY. (*Xing from down L. to up L., speaking
off L., as voices die out. She carries books under L.
arm*) I can't, Louise, I gotta go home. Goodbye.
(*Turns, facing down L.*) Oh, Ernestine! Ernestine!
Can you come over tonight and do Latin?— Isn't
that Cicero the worst thing?— Well, tell your
mother you have to. Goodbye. Goodbye, Helen,
goodbye, Fred. (*Turns few steps to up L. C.*)

GEORGE. (*Xing up to her, books under R. arm*)
Emily, can I carry your books home for you?

EMILY. (*Cooly*) Why—uh—thank you. It isn't
far. (GEORGE *takes her books under his left arm,
turns to speak off down L.* EMILY *is shy and embarrassed*)

GEORGE. 'Scuse me one minute, Emily, will

you?— (*Hurriedly*) Say, Bob, if I'm a little late, start practice, and give Herb some long high ones.

EMILY. (*Suddenly alert*) Goodbye, Lizzie.

GEORGE. (*Also to "LIZZIE", not enthusiastic*) Oh, goodbye. (BOTH *turn and stroll to up C.,* GEORGE *above,* BOTH *shy*) I'm awful glad you were elected too, Emily.

EMILY. (*Coldly*) Thank you. (*Stops up C. facing down. He stops R. of her*)

GEORGE. (*Hurt*) Emily, why are you mad at me?

EMILY. (*Defensive*) I'm not mad at you.

GEORGE. You've been treating me so funny lately.

EMILY. (*Dreading to face the issue*) Well, since you ask me, I might as well say it right out, George— (*Turns to him, catches sight of* TEACHER. *who has passed above to their R.*) Oh, goodbye, Miss Corcoran. (*Faces down again*)

GEORGE. (*Turning, then back*) Goodbye, Miss Corcoran.—Wha-what is it?

EMILY. (*Finding is very hard to say*) I don't like the whole change that's come over you in the last year. (GEORGE *turns R. a bit, hurt. She glances at him*) I'm sorry if that hurts your feelings; but I've just got to—tell the truth and shame the devil.

GEORGE. —A *change?*—Wha-what do you mean?

EMILY. (*Facing mostly out, on verge of tears*) Well, up to a year ago, I used to like you a lot. And I used to watch you while you did everything—because we'd been friends so long. And then you began spending all your time at baseball. (*She bites the word*) And you never stopped to speak to anybody any more—not to really speak—not even to your own family, you didn't. And George, it's a fact— ever since you've been elected Captain, you've got awful stuck up and conceited, and all the girls say so. And it hurts me to hear 'em say it; but I got to agree with 'em a little, because it's true.

GEORGE. (*Helpless and hurt*) Gosh, Emily—I

never thought that such a thing was happening to me—I guess it's hard for a fella not to have *some* faults creep into his character.

EMILY. (*The complete prig*) I always expect a man to be perfect and I think he should be.

GEORGE. Oh, I—I don't think it's possible to be perfect, Emily.

EMILY. (*All innocence, yet firm*) Well, my *father* is And as far as I can see, *your* father is. There's no reason on earth why you shouldn't be, too.

GEORGE. Well, I feel it's the other way round; that men aren't naturally good, but girls *are.*

EMILY. Well, you might as well know right now that *I'm* not *perfect.*—It's not as easy for a girl to be perfect as a man, because, well, we girls are more—nervous— (*Her face controls and she turns L.*) Now I'm sorry I said all that about you. I don't know what made me say it. (*Cries.*)

GEORGE. (*Choked voice*) Emily—

EMILY. Now I can see it's not the truth at all. And I suddenly feel that it's not important, anyway. (*Cries harder, hands to eyes*)

GEORGE. Emily—would you like an ice-cream soda, or something, before you go home?

EMILY. (*Controlling self*) Well, thank you—I—I would. (GEORGE *starts to take her arm, but is too shy. They start slowly down and turn into the drug-store R. C.*)

GEORGE. (*Over his emotions, as they walk, first gruffly, then courteously*) Hello, Stew, how are you?— Good afternoon, Mrs. Slocum. (*He starts R. into store, then steps back to let her go first*) (EMILY *Xes him to R. stool.* GEORGE *Xes to left end of board, puts books on it.*)

STAGE MANAGER. (*Enters down R., wearing glasses as* MR. MORGAN, *Xes to R. end of board*) Hello, George. Hello Emily. What'll you have?— Why, Emily Webb, what you been cryin' about?

GEORGE. (*Quickly Xing to her side as she looks to him for help*) She got an awful scare, Mr. Morgan. That—that hardware-store wagon almost ran over her. Everybody says Tom Huckins drives like a crazy man. (EMILY *nods agreement*)

STAGE MANAGER. (*Xing down R. to draw water*) Here, take a good drink-a-water, Emily. (EMILY *and* GEORGE *sit on stools, respectively R. and L. embarrassed.* BOTH *looking front*) You look all shook up. I tell you, you got to look both ways before you cross Main Street these days. (*Sets glass before her, She sips*) Gets worse every year— What'll you have?

EMILY. (*Hardly able to speak*) I'll have a strawberry phosphate, Mr. Morgan.

GEORGE. No, no, Emily—have a soda with me.

EMILY. Well,—

GEORGE. Two strawberry ice-cream sodas, Mr. Morgan.

STAGE MANAGER. (*Xing down R., facing out, as he mixes two sodas*) Two strawberry ice-cream sodas, yes sir. Yes, sir,—I want to tell you,—there are two hundred and twenty-five horses in Grover's Corners this minute I'm talking to you. (GEORGE *and* EMILY *face front through all this, she with tears in eyes, he very upset*) State Inspector was in here yestiddy. And now they're bringing in these auto-mo-biles, best thing to do is just stay home. Why I can remember when dogs used to sleep in the middle of the street all day, and nothing ever come to disturb'm. (*Sets sodas before them*) There you are! (*Sees someone off down R.*) Yes, Mrs. Ellis, be with you in a minute. What can I do for you? (*Exits down R.*)

EMILY. (*Awed*) They're so expensive. (*Sips through straw*)

GEORGE. No, no—don't you think of that, Emily.

We're celebrating—our election— And then do you know what else I'm celebrating?

EMILY. N-no.

GEORGE. I'm celebrating because I've got a friend who tells me all the things that ought to be told me.

EMILY. (*Tearfully*) George, please don't think of that. I don't know why I said it. It's not true. You're—

GEORGE. (*With brief look at her*) No, Emily, you *stick* to it. I'm *glad* you spoke to me like you did. But you'll *see*. I'm going to change so quick— you bet I'm going to change. (*She sips, winking back tears*) And Emily, I want to ask you a favor.

EMILY. W-wh-a-t?

GEORGE. Emily, if I go away to State Agriculture College next year, (*The thought hurts* EMILY *and she turns down R. biting lip*) will you write me a letter once in a whiie?

EMILY. (*Winks back tears*) I certainly will. I certainly will, George— (*Sips*) It certainly seems like being away three years you'd get out of touch with things. Maybe letters from Grover's Corners wouldn't be so interesting after a while. Grover's Corners isn't a very important place when you think of—all New Hampshire; but I think it's a very nice town. (*Sips*)

GEORGE. The day wouldn't come when I wouldn't want to know everything about our town. I know *that's* true. Emily—

EMILY. Well, I'll try to make the letters interesting. (*Pause*)

GEORGE. Y'know, Emily, whenever I meet a farmer I ask him if he thinks it's important to go to Agriculture School to be a good farmer.

EMILY. (*Looks at him, Happy that he may not leave town*) Why, George—

GEORGE. (*Eagerly*) Yeh, and some of them say

it's even a waste of time. (*She looks out down R., happy*) You can get all that stuff, anyway, in the pamphlets the Government sends out— And Uncle Luke's gettin' old,—he's about ready for me to start in taking over his farm tomorrow, if I could.

EMILY. (*Glowing*) My!

GEORGE. (*Front*) And like you say, being gone all that time—in other places and meeting other people—Gosh, if anything like that can happen I don't want to go away—I guess new people probably aren't any better than old ones. I'll bet they almost never are. Emily—I feel that you're as good a friend as I've got. I don't need to go and meet the people in other towns.

EMILY. (*To him, arguing nobly against her inclinations*) But George, maybe it's very important for you to go and learn all that,—about cattle-judging and soils and those things. (*Adding feebly*) Of course, I don't know.

GEORGE. (*After a pause—very serious*) Emily I'm going to make up my mind right now—I won't go. I'll tell Pa about it tonight.

EMILY. Why George. I don't see why you have to decide right now— It's a whole year away. (*Turns away, biting lip*)

GEORGE. Emily, I'm *glad* you spoke to me about that—that fault in my character. What you said was right; but there was one thing wrong in it. That's where you said that I wasn't noticing—people—and you, for instance—why, you say you were watchin' me when I did everything— Why, I was doing the same about you all the time. (*She looks at him wide-eyed, he at her*) Why sure—I always thought about you as one of the chief people I thought about. (*She turns away, joyously tearful*) I always made sure where you were sitting on the bleachers, and who you were with, and for three days not I've tried to walk home with you; but something's always got in the way. Yesterday, I was standing over by the wall waiting for you, (*Almost weeping*) and you walked home with Miss Corcoran.

EMILY. (*Breaking down a moment*) Oh, George!— Life's awful funny! (*Almost pleading*) How could I have known that? I thought—

GEORGE. Listen, Emily, I'm going to tell you why I'm not going to Agricultural School. I think once you've found a person you're very fond of—I mean a person who's fond of you, too, and who likes you well enough to be interested in your character— (EMILY *turns down R., terribly embarrassed*) Well, I think that's just as important as college is, and even more so. That's what I think.

EMILY. (*Quietly*) I think that's awfully important, too. (*Pause*)

GEORGE. Emily—

EMILY. Y—yes, George.

GEORGE. (*His head down. Squirming*) Emily, if I do improve, and make a big change,—would you be—I mean: could you be—

EMILY. (*Bursting into tears*) I—I am now; and I always have been.

GEORGE. (*Pause*) So I guess—this is an important talk we've been having— (*Snuffs*)

EMILY. Yes—yes. (*Pause. He suddenly dives into his soda, she into hers*)

GEORGE. (*Deep breath; straightens*) Wait just a minute and I'll walk you home. (BOTH *rise*, EMILY *Xes to wait by chair, R. of up C. facing up.* STAGE MANAGER *enters down R., Xes to table.* GEORGE *Xes to front of* EMILY's *stool*) Mr. Morgan, I'll— I'll have to go home and get the money to pay you for this.

STAGE MANAGER. (*Pretending annoyance*) What's that? George Gibbs, do you mean to tell me—!

GEORGE. Yes. But I had reasons, Mr. Morgan.

Look— (*Takes watch from trouser watch-pocket, holds it out to* STAGE MANAGER) here's my gold watch to keep until I come back with the money.

STAGE MANAGER. That's all right, George. Keep you watch. I'll trust you.

GEORGE. I'll be back in five minutes.

STAGE MANAGER. I'll trust you ten years, George —not a day over.— (GEORGE *slowly gets the point —laughs, returns watch, gets book under R. arm, starts up to* EMILY) Got all over your shock, Emily?

EMILY. (*Turns, step a bit L.*) Yes, thank you, Mr. Morgan—it was nothing.

GEORGE. (*Turning by her side*) I'm ready. (BOTH *walk down C. and off through trellis down L., very straight and radiant, but not looking at each other*)

STAGE MANAGER. (*Watches them off, then removes glasses and puts them in pocket, Xes C.*) Well, (*Claps hands*) now we'll get on to the wedding.

(*Immediately the lights except a pinspot which covers him fade out. Two* ASSISTANT STAGE MANAGERS *during the following speech remove the trellises, tables and the bench, and set thirty-two chairs facing up, sixteen on either side of an aisle, in close formation to suggest the pews of a church, four chairs to a row. They also set up C. a box for a pulpit and an extra chair R. of the first row for* SIMON STIMSON)

STAGE MANAGER. There are a lot of things to be said about a wedding. There are a lot of thoughts that go on during a wedding. We can't get them all into one wedding, naturally,—especially not into a wedding at Grover's Corners, where weddings are mighty short and plain. In this play I take the part of the minister. That gives me the right to say a few things more. Yes, for a while now the play gets pretty serious. Y'see,—some churches say that marriage is a sacrament. I don't quite know what that means, but I can guess. Like Mrs. Gibbs said a few minutes ago: people are supposed to live two-by-two. This is a good wedding. The people are pretty young, but they come from a good State, and they chose right. The real hero of this scene isn't on the stage at all. And you all know who that is. Like one of those European fellas said: Every time a child is born into the world it's Nature's attempt to make a perfect human being. Well, we've seen Nature pushing and contriving for some time now. We all know she's interested in quantity; but I think she's interested in quality, too. Maybe she's tryin' to make another good Governor for New Hampshire. That's what Emily hopes. And don't forget the other witnesses at this wedding: the ancestors. Millions of them. Most of them set out to live two-by-two. Millions of them. Well, that's all my sermon. 'Twan't very long anyway. (*Turning upstage, he walks up the church aisle, then R. to stand R. of choir placed* for SIMON STIMSON)

(*On cue "sermon" the pinspot has started to fade out*)
(*On same cue CHURCH BELLS sound,—ding-dong, ding-dong.*)
(*On sixth beat of bells enter from downstage sides of stage a* CROWD *of townspeople, who surge into the church, gradually lighted by dim lights crossing the stage from opposite rear corners. As townspeople crowd into the pews they are illumined from above. Then the* CHOIR *of ten stream in from R. and, facing down, take positions behind the pulpit. As they do so,* **strong lights flood the pulpit, the crosslights fade out, and the reflection of a slightly distorted church**

*window, "American Gothic" in style, is thrown
on the wall above the pulpit.)*
*(Entering with the crowd, MRS. GIBBS sits in the
first row, and seat on R.; MRS. WEBB in first
row, end seat on L. Next to them sit their hus-
bands, and next DOC GIBBS, REBECCA; next MR.
WEBB, WALLY. As the CHOIR gets into place,
the CHURCH BELLS stop and an unseen
ORGAN begins Handel's "Largo.")*

MRS. WEBB. *(At first note of music MRS. WEBB
rises. Xes down L. C., speaks)* I don't know why on
earth I should be crying. I suppose there's nothing
to cry about. This morning at breakfast it came over
me. There was Emily eating her breakfast as she's
done for seventeen years—and she's going out of
my house. I suppose that's it— And Emily! She
suddenly said: I can't eat another mouthful. And
she put her head on the table and *she* cried. Oh, I've
got to say it— You know, there's something down-
right cruel about sending girls out into marriages
like that. It's—it's cruel, I know; but I just couldn't
get myself to say anything—I went into it as blind
as a bat myself. The whole world's wrong, that's
what's the matter. *(Sees GEORGE coming down
stage-right aisle through audience)* There they
come. *(Xes up to sit)*

*(Three young BALLPLAYERS enter from R. tor-
mentor on cue "wrong" and, just inside it, call
out to GEORGE as he comes slowly down aisle)*

BASEBALL PLAYER ONE. Eh, George! George!
Hsst-yaow!
BASEBALL PLAYER TWO. Yao-o-o!
BASEBALL PLAYER ONE. Look at him, fellas. He's
scared to death!
BASEBALL PLAYER TWO. Oh, George!

BASEBALL PLAYER THREE. George!

BASEBALL PLAYER TWO. You don't have to look so innocent, you old geezer. We know what you're thinking.

BASEBALL PLAYER ONE. Go to it, big boy, y' old geezer you.

STAGE MANAGER. (*Xes down L. of them, pushes them off R.*) All right! All right! That'll do. That's enough of that.

BASEBALL PLAYERS. (*Tutti. Off.*) Yaou! Kee-ee. Whoo-oo-oo!

STAGE MANAGER. (*Steps to footlights, addresses audience*) There used to be an awful lot of that kind of thing in weddings in the old days,—Rome, and later— We're more civilized now,—so they say. (*Xes up R., across in front of choir to up R. and off down R.*)

(*As he starts up,* MRS. SOAMES *hurries in from behind tormentor to centre aisle of church, flutters a moment, sits in aisle on R. side of downstage row*)

(GEORGE, *having come down stage-right aisle through audience, has mounted steps over footlights and now stands R. of them surveying the scene, frightened*)

(*As* GEORGE *steps onto stage, the* ORGAN *and choir start "Love Divine, All Love Excelling", of which they do one verse, holding hymnals*)

MRS. GIBBS. (*Turning, sees him, hurries down to L. of him*) George! George! George! What's the matter?

GEORGE. Ma, I don't want to grow *old!* Why's everybody *pushing* me so?

MRS. GIBBS. Why, George—you wanted it.

GEORGE. No, Ma, listen to me—

MRS. GIBBS. No, no, George—you're a man now!

GEORGE. Listen, Ma—for the last time I ask you. All I want to do is to be a fella—

MRS. GIBBS. George! If anyone should hear you! Now stop! Why, I'm ashamed of you!

GEORGE. (*Calms down. Pause. He raises his head and looks over the scene*) What? Where's Emily?

MRS. GIBBS (*Relieved*) George, you gave me such a turn.

GEORGE. Cheer up, Ma. I'm getting married.

MRS. GIBBS. Let me catch my breath a minute.

GEORGE. (*Following, takes her arms, comforts her*) Now, Ma, you save Thursday nights. Emily and I are coming over to dinner every Thursday night—you'll see. Why, Ma, you look all funny. What are you crying for? Come on. We got to get ready for this. (MRS. GIBBS *controls herself and, as he continues to comfort her, fixes his tie, smooths his hair, and kisses him*)

(EMILY, *having come down the stage-left aisle through the audience, has stepped over the foot-lights, during* GEORGE'S *speech. She too looks over the scene, frightened, and turns half-front*)

(*As* EMILY *appears the ORGAN and choir, finishing the first hymn, start two verses of "Blessed Be The Tie That Binds."*)

EMILY. I never felt so alone in my whole life. (MR. WEBB, *hearing her, rises and hurries to R. of her*) And George, over there—I *hate* him—I wish I were dead. Papa! Papa! (*Flings herself in his arms*)

MR. WEBB. Emily! Emily! Now don't get upset—

EMILY. But, Papa darling,—I don't want to get married—

MR. WEBB. Sh-h—Emily—Everything's all right.

EMILY. (*Pleading*) Why can't I stay for a while just as I am? Let's go away—

MR. WEBB. No, no, Emily— Now stop and think a minute.

EMILY. Don't you remember what you used to say—all the time, that I was *your* girl. There must be lots of places we can go to. I'd work for you. I could keep house.

MR. WEBB. Sh! You musn't think of such things. You're just nervous. Now, now,— (*Turns R.*) George! George! Will you come here a minute! (*Takes her C. arms about her*) Why, you're marrying the best young fellow in the world. George is a fine fellow.

EMILY. But, Papa— (GEORGE, *on being called, gives a final pat to* MRS. GIBBS *and Xes to meet them C.* MRS. GIBBS *Xes up slowly to sit, now in control of herself.* MR. WEBB, *arms about* EMILY, *put his hand on* GEORGE'S *shoulder*)

MR. WEBB. I'm giving away my daughter, George. Do you think you can take care of her?

GEORGE. (*Trembling*) Mr. Webb, I want to—I want to try— (MR. WEBB *turns to face up, blows his nose.* EMILY *and* GEORGE *face each other, helpless, breathless.*) Emily, I'm going to do my best. I love you, Emily. I need you.

EMILY. Well, if you love me, help me—all I want is someone to love me.

GEORGE. I will, Emily, Emily, I'll try.

EMILY. And I mean for *ever*. Do you hear? For ever and ever. (*She flings her arms about his neck; his go about her waist in a long embrace*)

(*Hymn finishes and the ORGAN starts the "Wedding March from Lohengrin".*)

MR. WEBB. (*Turns and takes* EMILY'S *R. arm*) Come, they're waiting for us. Now, you know it'll be all right. Come quick.

(EMILY *and* MR. WEBB *slowly X up the church aisle.* STAGE MANAGER *has started from down L., at first note of the March. Xes up to mount box up C.* GEORGE, *as* MR. WEBB *takes* EMILY, *Xes front of them past L. of church to stand by* STAGE MANAGER, *just L. of him. Just after he reaches there,* MR. WEBB *arrives with* EMILY, *leaves her facing* GEORGE, *R. of pulpit, and goes to his seat*)

(*The* CROWD *has bustled with interest during the March, and is now all attention.*)

STAGE MANAGER. (*Hands holding lapels*) Do you, George, take this woman, Emily, to be your wedded wife, to have and to hold from this day forward, in sickness and in health, for richer for poorer, to love and to cherish till death do us part?

(*His voice sinks to an unintelligible mumble, over which rises the gabbling voice of* MRS. SOAMES)

MRS. SOAMES. (*On cue* "EMILY", *playing over* STAGE MANAGER, *to her neighbor*) Perfectly lovely wedding! Loveliest wedding I ever saw. Oh, I do love a good wedding, don't you? Doesn't she make a lovely bride?

GEORGE. I do!

STAGE MANAGER. Do you, Emily, take this man, George, to be your wedded husband, to have and to hold—etc.

MRS. SOAMES. (*On cue* "GEORGE") Don't know *when* I've seen such a lovely wedding. But I always cry; (*Wiping tears*) don't know why it is, but I always cry. I just like to see young people *happy.* Don't you? Oh, I think it's *lovely!*

EMILY. (*On cue* "happy") I do.

(STAGE MANAGER *mutters "The ring."* GEORGE
takes it from pocket, slips it on EMILY'S *finger,
then steps to embrace and kiss her. Kiss is held
throughout following speech,* EMILY'S *ecstatic
face uplifted against* GEORGE'S *L. shoulder*)

STAGE MANAGER. (*To audience*) I've married two
hundred couples in my day. Do I believe in it? I
don't know. I suppose I do. M marries N. Millions
of them. The cottage, the go-cart, the Sunday afternoon drives in the Ford—the first rheumatism—the
grandchildren—the second rheumatism—the death-
bed—the reading of the will— Once in a thousand
times it's interesting.

(*The ORGAN starts "Mendelssohn's Wedding
March". CHURCH BELLS sound*)
(GEORGE *and* EMILY *break, turn slowly down, smiling happily, and go slowly down aisle as lights
flood on them. They cross to R. steps, increasing speed, descend steps into theatre aisle and
run off in an increasing blaze of light. The*
TOWNSPEOPLE *have gradually risen and turned
to watch as they passed by, chattering.*)

MRS. SOAMES. (*As "Wedding March" starts*)
Aren't they a lovely couple? Oh, I've never been to
such a nice wedding, I'm sure they'll be happy. I
always say: Happiness—that's the great thing. The
important thing is to be *happy*.

(STAGE MANAGER, *as couple cross to steps, Xes
down C. All stage lights except window have
dimmed out as the couple crossed the footlights,
so that he now stands alone in a pinspot.*)

STAGE MANAGER. That's all the second act, folks.
Ten minutes intermission.

(*Pinspot and window go out.* STAGE MANAGER *in
     momentary darkness walks off R. The* CROWD
     exists R. and L.)
(*Pilot light fades in, followed by the house lights*)

END OF ACT TWO

ACT THREE

One minute after the end of Act II, two ASSISTANT
STAGE MANAGERS *clear the chairs and pulpit
box and set chairs for Act III.*
*At end of intermission, the following enter single
file, row by row, and sit (see ground plan for
seating order), entering in sequence as follows:*
WALLY, FARMER MCCARTHY, MRS. SOAMES,
2ND DEAD MAN, 1ST DEAD MAN, 1ST DEAD
WOMAN, 2ND DEAD WOMAN, MRS. GIBBS, *and*
SIMON STIMSON. *They remain placid throughout the act, facing out mostly, only half-turning
their heads to each other as they speak.*
*As they are mostly sected the house slowly dims and
the stage lights are slowly established.*
STAGE MANAGER *appears down R., lighted by his
pinspots. He no longer lounges, but stands near
the proscenium, hands behind him.*

STAGE MANAGER. This time nine years have gone
by, friends—summer, 1913. Gradual changes in
Grover's Corners. Horses are gettin' rarer. Farmers
coming into town now in Fords. Everybody locks
their house doors now at night. Ain't been any
burglars in town yet, but everybody's heard about
'em. You'd be surprised though—on the whole,
things don't change much around here— This is certainly an important part of Grover's Corners. It's on
a hilltop—a windy hilltop—lots of sky, lots of
clouds,—often lots of sun and moon and stars. You
come up here on a fine afternoon and you can see
range on ran of hills—awful blue they are—up
there by Lake Sunapee and Lake Winnipesaukee—

and if you go way up, you can see the White Mountains and Mount Washington—where North Conway and Conway is. And, of course, our favorite mountain, Mount Monadnock's right here—and all around it lie these towns—Jaffrey 'n North Jaffrey, 'n Peterborough, 'n Dublin and (*Then pointing down in the audience*) there, quite a way's down, is Grover's Corners. Yes, beautiful spot up here. Mountain laurel and li-lacks. I often wonder why people like to be buried in Woodlawn and Brooklyn when they might pass the same time up here in New Hampshire. (*Xing to L. C., pointing down L.*) Over here are the old stones—1660–1670. Strong-minded people that come a long ways to be independent. Summer people walk around there laughing at the funny words on the tombstones—it don't do any harm. And genealogists come up from Boston—get paid by city people for looking up their ancestors. They want to make sure they're Daughters of the American Revolution and of the Mayflower— Well, I guess that don't do any harm, either. Over there— (*down L. C.*) are some Civil War veterans. Iron flags on their graves— New Hampshire boys—had a notion that the Union ought to be kept together, though they'd never seen more than fifty miles of it themselves. All they knew was the name, friends— the United States of America. The United States of America. And they went and died about it. (*Xing three steps R.*) This here is the new part of the cemetery. There's your friend, Mrs. Gibbs, and Mr. Stimson, organist at the Congregational Church. And Mrs. Soames who enjoyed the weddin' so much, remember? Oh, and a lot of others. And Editor Webb's boy, Wallace, whose appendix burst while he was on a Boy Scout trip to Crawford Notch. (*Xing slowly down R.*) Yes, an awful lot of sorrow has sort of quieted down up here. People just wild with grief have brought their relatives up to this

hill—and then times—sunny days—rainy days—
snow— We all know how it is. A lot of thoughts
come up here, night and day, but there's no post
office— Now there are some things we all know but
we don't take'm out and look at'm very often. We all
know that *something* is eternal. And it ain't houses
and it ain't names, and it ain't earth, and it ain't
even the stars—everybody knows in their bones that
something is eternal, and that something has to do
with human beings. All the greatest people ever
lived have been telling us that for five thousand
years and yet you'd be surprised how people are always letting go of that fact. There's something way
down deep that's eternal about every human being.
(*Pause*) Y'know, the dead don't stay interested in
us living people for very long. Gradually, gradually,
they let go hold of the earth—and the ambitions
they had—and the pleasures they had—and the
things they suffered—and the people they loved.
They get weaned away from earth—that's the way I
put it, weaned away. Yes, they stay here while the
earth-part of 'em burns away, burns out, and all that
time they slowly get indifferent to what's goin' on
in Grover's Corners. They're waitin'. They're waitin'
for something they feel is comin'. Something important and great. Aren't they waitin' for the eternal
part in them to come out—clear? Some of the things
they're going to say maybe'll hurt your feelings—
but that's the way it is: mother 'n daughter—husband 'n wife—enemy 'n enemy—money 'n miser—
all those terribly important things kinda grow pale
around here. And what's left? What's left when
memory's gone, and your identity, Mrs. Smith?

(*Pause. Then* JOE STODDARD, *60-odd, enters from
down L. Xing to glance at grave a moment, then
turns L. downstage a bit and stands watching for
mourners off L. He carries his hat. At the same time*

enter up R. SAM CRAIG, *30, somewhat more citified than others in the play, carrying a rolled umbrella (real). He Xes rear of* DEAD *and down to R. of* JOE.) Well, here are some living people. There's Joe Stoddard, our undertaker, supervising a new-made grave. And here comes Sam Craig, a Grover's Corners boy that left town to go out West. (Watches them a moment, then strolls off down R.)*

SAM. (*Pleasantly*) Good afternoon, Joe Stoddard.

JOE. (*Turns surprised*) Good afternoon, good afternoon. Let me see now: do I know you?

SAM. I'm Sam Craig.

JOE. Gracious sakes' alive! Of all people! I shoulda knowed you'd be back for the funeral. You've been away a long time, Sam.

SAM. Yes, I've been away over twelve years. I'm in business out in Buffalo now, Joe— But I was in the East when I got news of my cousin's death, so I thought I'd combine things a little and come back and see the old home— You look well.

JOE. Yes, yes, can't complain— Very sad, our journey today, Samuel.

SAM. Yes. (*Xing up a bit to glance at grave*)

JOE. Yes, yes. I always say, I hate to supervise when a young person is taken. (SAM *turns R. glancing at gravestones, Xing to* MCCARTHY. JOE *looks off L.*) They'll be here in a few minutes now. I had to come here early today— (*Turns R.*) my son's supervisin' at the home.

SAM. (*As if reading stone. Reminiscing*) Old Farmer McCarthy! I used to do chores for him after school. He had lumbago. (*Xing slowing to L. of* MRS. GIBBS, *above her*)

JOE. Yes, we brought Farmer McCarthy here a number of years ago now.

SAM. Why, this is my Aunt Julia—I'd forgotten that she'd—of course, of course!

JOE. (*Xing R. a bit*) Yes, Doc Gibbs lost his wife

two-three years ago—about this time. And today's
another bad blow for him, too.

MRS. GIBBS. (*To* STIMSON: *in a pleasant tone*)
That's my sister Carrie's boy Sam—Sam Craig.

STIMSON (*Resentful*) I'm always uncomfortable
when *they're* around.

MRS. GIBBS. (*Gently*) Simon!

SAM. Do they choose their own verses much, Joe?

JOE. No—not usual. Mostly the bereaved pick a
verse.

SAM. (*Xing beyond* STIMSON) Doesn't sound like
Aunt Julia. Well, there aren't many of those Hersey
sisters left now, I suppose. (*Turns L.*) Let me see:
I wanted to look at my father's and mother's— (*His
eye falls on* STIMSON'S *stone*)

JOE. (*Points off R.*) Over there with the Craigs
—Avenue F.

SAM. (*After glance at* JOE, *focuses on* STIMSON)
He was organist at church, wasn't he? Drank a lot,
we used to say.

JOE. (*Xing to L. of* STIMSON, *above him*) Nobody was supposed to know about it. He'd seen a
peck of trouble. (*Glances L., confiden·ially*) Took
his own life, y'know?

SAM. Oh, did he?

JOE. Hung himself in the attic. They tried to hush
it up, but of course it got around. Chose his own
epitaph. You can see it there. It ain't a verse exactly.
(*Turns L.*)

SAM. Why, it's just some notes of music—what
is it?

JOE. (*Xing slowly C., turning up coat collar*) Oh,
I wouldn't know. It was wrote up in the Boston
papers at the time.

SAM. (*Follows*) Joe, what did she die of?

JOE. Who? (*Stops L. C. still looking off L.*)

SAM. My cousin. (*Stops C., opens umbrella*)

JOE. Oh, didn't you know? Had some trouble

bringing a baby into the world. 'Was her second, though. There's a little boy 'bout four years old.

SAM. And the grave's going to be over here— (*Xes to above grave*)

JOE. Yes, there ain't much more room over here among the Gibbses, so they're opening up a whole new Gibbs section over by Avenue B. You'll excuse me now. I see they're comin'. (*Xes off L., turns up and leads on the funeral procession, which is led by four bare-headed* MEN *carrying a coffin on their shoulders. Some twenty-five people follow after in groups and singly,* ALL *under umbrellas* (*real*). JOE *joins* SAM, *under his umbrella. The* PALLBEARERS *stop below the grave and set the coffin over it. The* OTHERS *all group in front of and L. of the grave, close-packed, their umbrellas hiding their heads.* MEN *remove hats as they near the grave.* EMILY *is in the crowd, a black cloak covering her white dress.*)

MRS. SOAMES. (*As procession moves on*) Who is it, Julia?

MRS. GIBBS. (*Without looking, pleasantly*) My daughter-in-law, Emily Webb.

MRS. SOAMES. (*A little surprised, but with no emotion*) Well, I declare! The road up here must have been awfully muddy. What did she die of, Julia?

MRS. GIBBS. (*Calmly*) In childbirth.

MRS. SOAMES. Childbrith! I'd forgotten all about that! My, wasn't life awful—(*With a sigh*) and wonderful.

STIMSON. (*Bitter*) Wonderful, was it?

MRS. GIBBS. Simon! Now, remember!

MRS. SOAMES. (*A bit surprised*) I remember Emily's wedding. Wasn't it a lovely wedding! And I remember her reading the class poem at Graduation Exercises. Emily was one of the brightest girls ever graduated from High School. I've heard Principal Wilkins say so time after time. I called on

them at their new farm, just before I died. Perfectly
beautiful farm.

(FUNERAL GROUP *is now in place*)

1ST DEAD WOMAN. It's on the same road we lived
on, hm-hm.
1ST DEAD MAN. Aya, right smart farm.

(*The* GROUP *by the grave sings softly and slowly one
verse of "Blessed Be The Tie That Binds."*)

2ND DEAD WOMAN. I always liked that hymn. I
was hopin' they'd sing a hymn. (*Two beats after the
first line of the hymn,* EMILY, *in her wedding dress
without the veil, emerges swiftly up C. from behind
the group; stops after a few steps to look at the*
DEAD, *first with surprise then with understanding;
turns to survey the funeral group lovingly, stretches
arms toward them, then slowly walks to the chair
left vacant for her, and sits facing out. Then she
turns to the dead*)
EMILY. (*To all* DEAD, *quietly*) Hello!
MRS. SOAMES. (*Looking straight out*) Hello,
Emily!
1ST DEAD MAN. (*Out*) H'lo, M's Gibbs!
EMILY. (*Warmly*) Hello, Mother Gibbs!
MRS. GIBBS. Emily!

(A VOICE *in the* FUNERAL GROUP *mumbles a
portion of the funeral service, but the words are
inaudible.*)

EMILY. Hello! (*Faces front. Pause, she looks out
and up,—surprised*) It's raining! (*She looks at
funeral*)
MRS. GIBBS. (*Facing front throughout*) Yes—
They'll be gone soon, dear. Just rest yourself.

EMILY. It seems thousands and thousands of years since I— (*The prayer over, the* FUNERAL GROUP *sings Second verse of "Blessed Be The Tie That Binds."*) (*Pleased*) Papa remembered that that was my favorite hymn. (*Pause—turns slowly R.*) Oh, I wish I'd been here a long time! I don't like being new here. (*Leans forward*) Oh, how do you do, Mr. Stimson?

SIMON STIMSON. (*Firmly*) How do you do, Emily?

EMILY. (*His tone confuses her a moment*) (*Settling back for the first time, more at ease. Enthusiastic*) Mother Gibbs, George and I have made that farm into just the best place you ever saw. We thought of you all the time. We wanted to show you the new barn and a great long ce-ment drinking fountain for the stock. We bought that out of the money you left us.

MRS. GIBBS. I did?

EMILY. Don't you remember, Mother Gibbs—the legacy you left us? Why, it was over three hundred and fifty dollars.

(*Starting with those at L. the* FUNERAL GROUP *breaks up and exits slowly L. A* SMALL GROUP *only remains at grave,—*MR. *and* MRS. WEBB, GEORGE, *and* DR. GIBBS, *who has no umbrella*)

MRS. GIBBS. Yes, yes, Emily.

EMILY. Well, there's a pa-tent device on this drinking-fountain so that it never overflows, Mother Gibbs, and it never sinks below a certain mark they have there. It's fine. (*Her voice trails off and her eyes return to the funeral. Sadly:*) It won't be the same to George without me, but it's a lovely farm. (*Looks front again, sits forward, struck by a new realization*) Live people don't understand, do they?

MRS. GIBBS. No, dear—not very much.

EMILY. They're sort of shut up in little boxes, aren't they? I feel as tho I knew 'em last a thousand years ago— (*Sits back, again at ease, easily*) My boy is spending the day at Mrs. Carter's. (*Turns to 1st DEAD MAN*) (*The CROWD is now off*) Oh, Mr. Carter, my little boy is spending the day at your house.

1ST DEAD MAN. Is he?

EMILY. Yes, he loves it there. Mother Gibbs, we have a Ford, too. (MR. *and* MRS. WEBB *and* GEORGE *slowly exeunt L.*) Never gives any trouble. I don't drive, though. (*Pause*) (*Pained,—sitting forward*) Mother Gibbs, when does this feeling go away?—Of being one of *them?* How long does it—

MRS. GIBBS. Sh! dear. Just wait and be patient.

(DR. GIBBS *kneels to take flowers from grave, slowly rises and crosses to face* MRS. GIBBS)

EMILY. (*Looking off L., calmly*) I know— Look, they're finished. They're going.

MRS. GIBBS. Sh-h-h!

EMILY. (*Lovingly*) Look! Father Gibbs is bringing some of my flowers to you. (*As he passes, surprised*) He looks just like George, doesn't he? (DR. GIBBS *lays flowers at wife's feet and stands, head bowed and sighs*) (*All sympathy:*) Oh, Mother Gibbs, I never realized before how troubled and how —how in the dark live persons are. Look at him. I loved him so. (*Long pause. DR. GIBBS exits slowly L., gradually raising head. When he is two-thirds off, and putting on his hat*) From morning till night, that's all they are—troubled.

1ST DEAD MAN. (*Colloquially*) Little cooler than it was.

1ST DEAD WOMAN. Aya, that rain's cooled it off a little.

1ST DEAD MAN. Those northeast winds always

do the same thing, don't they? If 'tain't a rain, it's a three-day blow.

EMILY. (*Sitting up abruptly, her L. hand hugging her waist, both fists clenched*) But Mother Gibbs, one can go back; one can go back there again—into living! I feel it! I know it! Why just then for a moment I was thinking about—about the farm—and for a minute I was *there* (*Looking at her lap a moment*) and my baby was on my lap as plain as day!

MRS. GIBBS. Yes, of course you can.

EMILY. (*Excited*) I can go back there and live all those days over again—why not?

MRS. GIBBS. All I can say is, Emily, don't. (STAGE MANAGER *enters down R. and stands hands behind him, looking out.*)

EMILY. (*To* STAGE MANAGER, *but only half facing him*) But it's true, isn't it? I can go and live—back there—again.

STAGE MANAGER. (*Quietly*) Yes, some have tried, but they soon come back here.

MRS. GIBBS. (*Gently*) Don't do it, Emily.

MRS. SOAMES. (*Pleading*) Emily, don't. It's not what you think it'd be.

EMILY. (*Eagerly*) But I won't live over a sad day. I'll choose a happy one— I'll choose the day I first knew that I loved George! (*Leans forward as in pain, pressing L. arm to side*) Oh no, no! Why should that be painful?

STAGE MANAGER. You not only live it; but you watch yourself living it.

EMILY. (*Head up, still leaning forward*) Yes?

STAGE MANAGER. And as you watch it, you see the thing that they—down there—never know. You see the future. You know what's going to happen afterwards.

EMILY. (*Sitting up*) But is that—painful? Why?

MRS. GIBBS. That's not the only reason why you shouldn't do it, Emily. When you've been here longer you'll see that—- Our life here is to forget all that— (EMILY *shakes her head*) and think only of what is ahead—and be ready for what is ahead. When you've been here longer you'll understand.

EMILY. But, Mother Gibbs, how can I *ever* forget *that* life? It's all I know! It's all I had!

MRS. SOAMES. Oh, Emily! It isn't wise. Really, it isn't.

EMILY. (*Insistent*) But it's a thing I must know for myself! I'll choose a happy day, anyway.

MRS. GIBBS. (*Sharply*) No! (*Calmly*) At least, choose an unimportant day. Choose the least important day in your life. It will be important enough.

EMILY. (*To herself*) Then it can't be since I was married; or since the baby was born. (*To* STAGE MANAGER, *eagerly*) I can choose a birthday at least, can't I?—I choose my twelfth birthday.

STAGE MANAGER. All right. It's February 11th, 1899. A Tuesday. Do you want any special time of day?

EMILY. Oh, I want the whole day!

STAGE MANAGER. We'll begin at dawn. You remember it had been snowing for several days; but it stopped the night before, and they had begun clearing the roads. (EMILY *rises, turns up L.*) The sun's coming up. (*The wall area up L., followed by the area of the Webb kitchen, glows with light*)

EMILY. (*With a cry of amazement, Xing a bit C.*) There's Main Street—why, that's Mr. Morgan's drugstore before he changed it! . . . (*Xing up L. C., with brief—surprised look back at* STAGE MANAGER) And there's the livery stable!

STAGE MANAGER. Yes, it's 1899. This is fourteen years ago.

EMILY. (*Amazed*) Oh, that's the town I knew as a little girl! (*Faces—turns down—warmly*) And, look, there's the old white fence that used to be around our house. Oh, I'd forgotten that! I love it

SO! (*She almost embraces it, then turns eagerly to* STAGE MANAGER) Are *they* inside?

STAGE MANAGER. Yes, your mother'll be coming downstairs in a minute to make breakfast.

EMILY. (*Softly*) Will she?

STAGE MANAGER. And you remember: your father had been away for a couple of days; he came back on the early morning train.

EMILY. No?

STAGE MANAGER. He'd been back to his college to make a speech—in Western New York, at Clinton.

EMILY. (*Trying to remember, turns thoughtfully L.*) Look! There's Howie Newsome! (*Xing a bit L.*) There's our policeman! (*Looks at* STAGE MANAGER, *confused*) But he's *dead;* he *died!*

HOWIE. (*Off L.*) Whoa, Bessie!—Morning, Bill.

BILL. (*Off L.*) Morning, Howie.

HOWIE. You're up early.

(EMILY, *listening in delight, turns slowly towards them*)

BILL. Been rescuin' a party; darn near froze to death, down by Polish Town thar. Got drunk and lay out in the snowdrifts. (*They laugh*) Thought he was in bed when I shook'm.

EMILY. (*Delighted*) There's Joe Crowell!

(*Enter* MRS. WEBB *from L., unnoticed by* EMILY, *Xing briskly front of her to shake grate of stove*)

JOE CROWELL. (*Off down L.*) Good mornin', Mr. Warren. 'Mornin', Howie.

CONSTABLE WARREN AND HOWIE. Mornin', Joe.

MRS. WEBB. (*Turning L. at stove*) Children! Wally! Emily! Time to get up! (*Turns to stove and quickly adds coal to fire*)

EMILY. (*Has turned excitedly on hearing her mother's voice, and now hurries behind her to up R. of her*) (*In ecstasy*) Mama, I'm here! (*Gently*) Oh, how young Mama looks! I didn't know Mama was ever that young—

(HOWIE, *starting down L. on "time to get up" to usual sound of MILK BOTTLES, has crossed up C. and is now coming down to where trellis stood down L.*)

MRS. WEBB. (*Xing to where stairs previously were—calling upstairs*) You can come and dress by the kitchen fire, if you like, but hurry. (*Hurries to meet* HOWIE *down L.*) Good mornin', Mr. Newsome.

HOWIE NEWSOME. Mornin', Mis' Webb. (*Handing her two bottles of milk*)

MRS. WEBB. (*Clutching sweater at neck*) Whhh —it's cold.

HOWIE. (*Starting up C. and then off R.*) Yep. Ten below by my barn, Mis' Webb.

(*As* HOWIE *passes by her to up C.,* EMILY *turns and reaches out her arms to him, craving to embrace him*)

MRS. WEBB. (*Calling after him*) Think of it! Keep yourself wrapped up. (*Picks up album, drops it on table and takes bottles to table above stove. From this point on she moves no more than two short steps from stove, suggesting movements about kitchen rather than pacing them*)

HOWIE. (*As he exits*) Come on, Bessie, gid-ap!

EMILY. (*Turns to her mother, makes up her mind half-fearfully to speak*) Mama, I can't find my blue hair-ribbon anywhere.

MRS. WEBB. (*Turning at stove to call upstairs*) Just open your eyes, dear, that's all, I laid it out for you special on the dresser, there. If it were a snake, it'd bite you. (*Turns to start breakfast at stove, her moves more confined and less realistic than in previous acts*)

EMILY. (*Smiling agreement as mother reacts as she hoped*) Yes—yes—

(MRS. WEBB *Xes to cupboard for dishes and silver, then to set table where it used to stand, making two quick trips*)

(CONSTABLE WARREN, *having started down L. on "blue hair ribbon", walking as though against a cold wind, has reached up C. MR. WEBB, starting down L. on "bite you", Xes up C. and then down as if through trellis, speaking as he starts and never stopping*)

MR. WEBB. Good mornin', Bill.

CONSTABLE WARREN. (*Stops up C. to look back*) Good mornin', Mr. Webb. You're up early.

(EMILY, *ecstatic at seeing her father, watches him from the moment he turns the corner up L., never taking her eyes from him. As he crosses down C. she follows him, reaching arms as if to grasp him and whispering "Papa!" but he keeps hurrying away from her to the trellis. She draws quickly up to above R. of her mother and watches the scene between mother and father eagerly*)

MR. WEBB. Yes, just been back to my old college in New York State. Been any trouble here?

CONSTABLE WARREN. (*Louder as MR. WEBB moves away*) I was called up this mornin' to rescue a Polish fella—darn near froze to death he was. (*Starts off R.*)

MR. WEBB. (*Calling back loudly*) We must get it in the paper.

(MRS. WEBB *Xes to putter at stove*)

CONSTABLE WARREN. Twan't much. (*Exits R.*)

MR. WEBB. (*Stamping snow from feet as he enters house*) Good mornin', Mother. (*Xes off L. to remove hat and coat*)

MRS. WEBB. (*At stove*) How did it go, Charles?

(EMILY *Xes slowly up L. of* MRS. WEBB, *watching in agonized delight*)

MR. WEBB. Oh, fine, I guess. I told 'em a few things. Everything all right here?

MRS. WEBB. Yes—can't think of anything that's happened, special. (MR. WEBB *returns, rubbing cold hands, stays L. of* EMILY) Been right cold. Howie Newsome says its ten below over to his barn.

MR. WEBB. Yes, well, it's colder than that at Hamilton College. Students' ears are falling off. It ain't Christian— (EMILY *smiles through tears at remembering the joke*) Paper have any mistakes in it?

MRS. WEBB. None that I noticed. (MR. WEBB *starts off L., then stops*) Coffee's ready when you want it. Charles! Don't forget; it's Emily's birthday. Did you remember to get her anything?

MR. WEBB. (*Hand on pocket*) Yes, I've got something here. (*Xing off L., calling gaily*) Where's my girl? Where's my birthday girl?

MRS. WEBB. Don't interrupt her now, Charles. You can see her at breakfast. She's slow enough as it is. Hurry up, children! Seven o'clock. Now I don't want to call you again. (*Turns to pare potatoes at table above stove, facing up*)

EMILY. (*Softly, rueful*) I can't bear it. They're so young and beautiful. Why did they ever have to get old? (*Xing to near mother, who turns down to putter at store*) Mama, I'm here! I'm grown up! I love you all, everything! (*Leans over table as if wanting to embrace it*) (MRS. WEBB *faces up, pares potatoes*) I can't look at everything hard enough. (*With a new eager thought, she looks at* STAGE MANAGER *and whispers lightly, "Can I go in?" He nods soberly. Smiling in anticipation, she turns a few steps up L., then down and R., as if entering kitchen, then beams at mother*) (*Gently, as a girl of 12*) Good morning, Mama.

MRS. WEBB (*Xing to embrace and kiss her— without showing her true affection*) Well, now, dear, a very happy birthday to my girl and many happy returns. (*Returns to stove, slipping out of* EMILY'S *arms, which were about to embrace her*) There are surprises waiting for you on the kitchen table.

EMILY. (*Terribly hurt at her mother's lack of emotion, looks down at her wedding-dress between her empty arms, then at her mother who is calmly puttering at the stove. Finally she forces herself to speak a banality:*) Oh, Mama, you shouldn't have. (*Looking for help from the unmoved* STAGE MANAGER, *she clasps her hands in agonized appeal toward him and, as she speaks, moves a couple of steps C.*) I can't! I can't!

MRS. WEBB. (*Over her shoulder, dryly as usual*) But birthday or no birthday, I want you to eat your breakfast good and slow. I want you to grow up and be a good strong girl. (EMILY *steps to "table", looks over gifts*) That in the blue paper is from your Aunt Carrie and I reckon you can guess who brought the post card album. I found it on the doorset when I brought in the milk— George Gibbs— must come over in the cold pretty early—right nice of him. (*Putters at stove again*)

EMILY. (*Very gently, picking up album*) Oh, George! I'd forgotten that— Oh!

MRS. WEBB. Chew that bacon good an' slow. It'll help keep you warm on a cold day.

EMILY. (*Unable to stand longer her mother's aloofness, slowly drops album on table, and moves quickly to L. of Mother*) (*Passionately*) Oh, Mama, just look at me one minute as though you really saw me. (MRS. WEBB *turns front to stir oatmeal at stove, placid and smiling, not hearing.* EMILY *turns down close behind her*) Mama! Fourteen years have gone by!— I'm dead!— You're a grandmother, Mama— (*More and more desperate*) I married George Gibbs, Mama!— Wally's dead, too.— Mama! His appendix burst on a camping trip to Crawford Notch. We felt just terrible about it, don't you remember?—(*More gently and appealing*) But, just for a moment now we're all together— Mama, just for a moment let's be happy— (*In greatest desperation*) Let's look at one another!

MRS. WEBB. (*One step L., to put dish on table*) That in the yellow paper is something I found in the attic among your grandmother's things. You're old enough to wear it now, and I thought you'd like it.

EMILY. (*Turns to table, forcing her child's tone*) And this is from you! Why, Mama, it's just lovely and it's just what I wanted. It's beautiful! (*She flings her arms around her mother's shoulders.* MRS. WEBB *pats her hand, then turns away to stove*)

MRS. WEBB. (*Pleased*) Well, I hoped you'd like it. (*As she turns away,* EMILY *is again agonized*) Hunted all over. Your Aunt Norah couldn't find one in Concord so I had to send all the way to Boston. (*Laughing*) Wally has something for you, too. (EMILY *turns L., stretching arms toward upstairs to* WALLY) He made it at Manual Training class and he's very proud of it. Be sure you make a big fuss about it. Your father has a surprise for you, too; don't know what it is myself. Sh—here he comes.

MR. WEBB. (*Off L.*) Where's my girl? Where's

my birthday girl? (*Swaying,* EMILY *turns up and to C., weeping, rushes rear of mother. As she does so, lights dim on house area, whereat* MRS. WEBB *exits sedately and slowly L.*)

EMILY. (*As she crosses to up C.*) I can't! I can't go on! (*Sobs a moment*) It goes so fast. We don't have time to look at one another. (*She breaks down sobbing again, controls herself and looks off down L.*) I didn't *realize.* So *all* that was going on and we never noticed! (*Half to* STAGE MANAGER, *Xing slowly down C.*) Take me back—up the hill—to my grave. But first: Wait! (*Turns L.*) One more look! (*Xing up L. C.*) (*Gently*) Goodbye! (*Then passionately, her arms outflung*) Goodbye, world! (*Then lovingly, glancing at the town up L.*) Goodbye, Grover's Corners— (*Turns to look off down L., softly*) Mama and Papa— (*Turns a step C., eyes uplifted*) Goodbye to clocks ticking—and my butternut tree! (*Her eyes follow its trunk down and she moves lovingly toward it a step or two, then gestures toward the garden*) and Mama's sunflowers— (*Her head gradually raised as the thrill grows*) and food and coffee—and new-ironed dresses and hot baths— (*With increasing fervor*) and sleeping and waking up!— (*She flings her arms wide in an ecstasy of realization*) Oh, earth, you're too wonderful for anyone to realize you! (*Thinking a moment, she half-turns to the* STAGE MANAGER, *questioning more gently:*) Do any human beings ever realize life while they live it—every, every minute?

STAGE MANAGER. (*Quietly*) No.— Saints and poets maybe—they do some. (*Pause*)

EMILY. (*Calmly, after absorbing the thought*) I'm ready to go back. (*Xes slowly to sit. As she does so, the lights dim up L., leaving only a deep blue except for amber on the dead*)

MRS. GIBBS. (*After a long pause, quietly*) Were you happy?

EMILY. No. I should have listened to you. (*Pityingly*) That's all human beings are!— Just blind people.

MRS. GIBBS. (*Gently and cheerfully, looking up and out*) Look, it's clearing up. The stars are coming out.

EMILY. (*After a glance up, turning slowly R.*) Oh, Mr. Stimson, I should have listened to them. (*She sits back at ease, nodding agreement as he speaks*)

STIMSON. (*With mounting violence*) Yes. Now you know. Now you know: that's what it *was* to be *alive*. To move about in a cloud of ignorance; to go up and down trampling on the feelings of those—of those about you. To spend and waste time as though you had a million years. To be always at the mercy of one self-centered passion, or another. Now you know—that's the "happy" existence you wanted to go back to. Ignorance and blindness!

MRS. GIBBS. (*Spiritedly*) That ain't the whole truth and you know it, Simon Stimson. (*Resuming her tranquility*) Emily, look at that star. I forget its name.

1ST DEAD MAN. (*Quietly, proud of his son*) My boy Joel was a sailor—knew 'em all. He'd set on the porch evenin's 'n tell 'em all by name. Yes, sir, wonderful.

2ND DEAD MAN. A star's mighty good company.

1ST DEAD WOMAN. Yes. Yes 'tis.

STIMSON. (*Resentfully, with a glance half L.*) There's one of *them* comin'.

2ND DEAD WOMAN. That's funny! 'Tain't no time for 'em to be here.

1ST DEAD WOMAN. Goodness sakes!

EMILY. (*Watching off down L.*) Mother Gibbs! It's George! (*GEORGE appears down L., hat in L. hand, crossing slowly front to face EMILY.*)

MRS. GIBBS. Sh-h, dear. Just rest yourself.

EMILY. (*Tenderly*) It's George!

1ST DEAD MAN. (*As before*) And my Joel, who knew the stars—he used to say it took millions of years for that little speck o' light to git down to earth. Don't seem like a body could believe it, but that's what he used to say—millions of years.

(GEORGE *slowly kneels before* EMILY, *drops hat, and slowly falls forward face on ground*)

1ST DEAD WOMAN. Goodness! That ain't no way to behave.

MRS. SOAMES. He ought to be home.

(GEORGE *gives a convulsive sob*)

EMILY. (*Softly, looking down at* GEORGE, *all pity*) Mother Gibbs?

MRS. GIBBS. Yes, Emily?

EMILY. They don't—understand—do they?

MRS. GIBBS. No, dear. They don't understand.

(*TRAIN WHISTLES off R.*)

STAGE MANAGER. (*Draws a blue traveller curtain from R. to L. speaking as he starts*) Most everybody's asleep in Grover's Corners. There are a few lights on: Shorty Hawkins, down at the depot, has just watched the Albany train go by. And at the livery stable somebody's setting up late and talking. —Yes, it's clearing up. (*Stops a moment, looking out and up*) There are the stars—doing their old, old criss-cross in the skies. (*Continues*) Scholars haven't settled the matter yet, but they seem to think there are no living beings up there. Just chalk—or fire. Only this one is straining away, straining away all the time to make something of itself. The strain's so great that every sixteen hours everybody lies down and gets a rest. (*CLOCK strikes. He reaches*

L.) Hm— Eleven o'clock in Grover's Corners. (*He winds his watch*) Everybody's resting in Grover's Corners. Tomorrow's going to be another day. You get a good rest too. Good night. (*Exits down L.*)

(*The traveller curtain opens slowly disclosing a completely empty and unlighted stage.*)

END OF THE PLAY

NOTE ON PANTOMIME

While it is impossible in the script to describe in complete detail the many moments of pantomime, some indications may be of service in reproducing it.

MRS. GIBBS' BREAKFAST starts by her raising the window shade, putting up window with both hands, turning to stove, lifting off lids with a handle-holder, putting holder down, placing kindling in stove from box beside it, taking match from box above stove, scratching it on box, lighting fire, replacing stove lids, etc.

MR. MORGAN'S MIXING OF SODAS starts with him taking two glasses from higher shelf and placing them on lower. He takes syrup bottle, removes stopper, pours into both glasses, replaces stopper and bottle. Takes one glass, turns right, removes lid from ice-cream receptacle, takes ice-cream scoop and puts cream into glass. Repeats with second glass, replaces lid of receptacle. Holds first glass up to soda faucet and turns old-fashioned wheel faucet. Sets glass down and repeats with second.

All pantomime should be worked out realistically and in at least sufficient detail so that the actor definitely knows what he is doing. If, however, the pantomime is too detailed, it will distract from the lines of the STAGE MANAGER or even from the actors who are pantomiming. A happy medium should be struck between pantomime which tells its own story and definitely underdone miming. In other words, it should be kept as a background effect.

NOTE ON WEDDING ENTRANCE

This can be one of the most effective movements in the play if properly handled. It should not be realistic, but merely a dignified entrance of actors getting into place.

The CONGREGATION should gather as near as possible to the Right and Left tormentors, lined up to follow each other as they are to sit in the "pews". On the sixth stroke of chimes (as the dim "wall lights" come up on their faces) the two people who are to sit in central-aisle seats of the second rows from the pulpit start slowly walking to the outer end om their "pews" and into place to sit. When they have progressed some five feet from the start, the persons leading the first (or family) and third lines start. When third-line leaders have progressed some five feet, those leading the fourth line start. In each case the leaders are followed at about three-foot distances by others in their "pews". This arrangement produces a wedge-like formation from either side, which, as the church lights gradually form (per light plot), is tremendously effective from the front.

By no means all the seats in the church need be filled. The congregation should remain unmoved, merely pictorial, except for two moments: (1) when the wedding-march starts they should move expectantly and gradually turn to watch the BRIDE pass up the aisle, and (2) as the COUPLE go down the aisle they should rise, chatting, and watch the COUPLE throughout the exit.

DOUBLING AND UNDERSTUDY PLOT

PROFESSOR WILLARD: Sings in choir, plays 1st DEAD MAN, understudies STAGE MANAGER and MR. WEBB.

WOMAN IN BALCONY: Sings in choir, plays 1st DEAD WOMAN, understudies MRS. WEBB, MRS. SOAMES.

MAN IN AUDITORIUM: Plays BASEBALL PLAYER, is ASSISTANT STAGE MANAGER, understudies GEORGE.

LADY IN THE BOX: Sings in choir, understudies MRS. GIBBS.

BASEBALL PLAYER: Is ASSISTANT STAGE MANABER, understudies SIMON STIMSON and SAM CRAIG.

FARMER MCCARTHY: Understudies CONSTABLE WARREN, JOE STODDARD, and 1st DEAD MAN.

STAGE MANAGER: Plays SAM CRAIG, understudies HOWIE NEWSOME and PROFESSOR WILLARD.

CHOIR SINGER: Understudies DOC GIBBS, and MAN IN AUDITORIUM.

CHOIR SINGER: Understudies EMILY and REBECCA, and LADY IN Box, and WOMAN IN BALCONY.

IF NO UNDERSTUDY IS ENGAGED FOR THREE BOYS:
In case of illness of JOE CROWELL, scene must be cut and STAGE MANAGER'S succeeding speech also cut.

WALLY understudies SI CROWELL (STAGE

MANAGER's introductory line being changed
accordingly to cover WALLY).

SI CROWELL understudies WALLY (with same
change in Act II)

BASEBALL PLAYERS can be reduced from three to
two without changes in lines.

Lines of 2ND DEAD WOMAN can be spoken by MRS.
SOAMES.

Lines of 2ND DEAD MAN can be spoken by FARMER
McCARTHY.

PROPERTY PLOT

Off Left

   16 assorted rehearsal chairs
    1 trellis, portable, with roses
   20 umbrellas, sprinkled with waterglass to simu-
       late rain
    1 cane (Constable Warren)
    1 table about 21" x 36"
    1 box about 11" x 20" x 14" for pulpit
    1 wooden piano bench
    1 stepladder, black, on wheels

Sound Effects:

      Train whistle
      Factory whistle
      Schoolbell
      Lawnmower (coffee ground in coffee mill
        off)
      Milk bottles (bottles in rack off)
      Cockcrow (vocal)
      Bobwhite (vocal)
      Crickets (vocal)
      Whinny (vocal)

    1 handkerchief for bandage (Mr. Webb)

Off Right

   16 assorted rehearsal chairs (2 with straight
      backs to be used L. of table R. C. for board
      in soda fountain scene; 1 with short legs
      for Wally in Act III)
    1 table about 2' square.
    1 prompt Mss (Stage Manager)
    1 pipe (Stage Manager)
    1 pocket watch (Stage Manager)
    2 stools (soda fountain)
    1 umbrella without waterglass (Sam Craig)
    1 organ
    1 baseball bat (1st Baseball Player)

1 baseball glove (2nd BASEBALL PLAYER)
1 8′ board (soda fountain scene)
1 stepladder wide enough for GEORGE *and* RE-
   BECCA, on wheels, black
1 trellis with vines
SOUND EFFECTS:
   Chickens (vocal)
   Thunder (thunder drum)
   Church chimes (pipes, C sharp and D)
   Town clock (use same)
   Newspapers (newspapers wrapped and
   skidded on floor)

ORCHESTRA PIT
   L portable organ
   2 benches to hold 5 people each
   1 box for Stimson to stand on

NOTE

The use of many props is indicated in this script,
but, except for those used by the Stage Manager
and for the umbrellas used in Act III, it must be
understood that all are imagined.

COSTUME PLOT

(In the original production the costumes were
designed for the 1901-1904 period without emphasis on what might prove the amusing ele-
ment.)
STAGE MANAGER—Worn gray suit. Old tan shoes.
   Gray felt hat. Coat worn open. Vest unbuttoned
   two top buttons. Spectacles for "Mr. Morgan."
MRS. GIBBS—Act I. Dark blue woolen dress. Blue
   striped waist. Flowered apron. Act II. Same,
   with gray knitted shawl. For wedding: add
   dark blue sailor hat and gray lace collar, and

dark blue tippet. Act III. Same as Act I minus apron.—For return from choir meeting, same with hat and lace collar. Low black shoes and gray cotton stockings throughout. Blond pompadour wig.

MRS. WEBB—Act I. Dark gray woolen skirt. Brown cotton waist. Blue checked kitchen apron. For return from choir practice, remove apron and add brown hat and lace collar. Act II. Same for first scene as at opening of Act I. For wedding add hat and green shoulder cape. Act III. For funeral, black cape, hat, and mourning veil. For later scene, blue sweater and apron over previous skirt and waist. Black shoes and gray cotton stockings throughout.

EMILY—Act I. Blue woolen jumper skirt. Light blue middy waist and black tie. Black hair bow. Gray woolen stockings and Mary Jane slippers. Act II. Flowered cotton print dress. Same bow and shoes, with white stockings. For wedding: white wedding dress and veil, with stiff muslin petticoat. White shoes. Act III. Same as for wedding minus veil, substituting limp cotton petticoat. Black floor-length cape for funeral entrance (given to an extra as she leaves group.)

MRS. SOAMES—Act I. Blue woolen skirt. Green plaid waist. Blue straw hat. Black Oxfords and gray stockings. Act II. Same with jabot added. Act III. Same as Act I minus hat.

DR. GIBBS—Acts I and II. Brown, loose-fitting, 3-button suit. Brown shoes and socks. Leghorn hat. Act III. Dark overcoat and gray felt hat. Throughout: white shirt, low turnover collar, black string tie.

MR. WEBB—Act I. Gray tweed suit. Light gray checked vest. Blue shirt with white turnover collar. Black bow tie. Handkerchief held around right middle finger as bandage. Armbands to show when mowing lawn. Final scene in act; gray soft hat. Act II: Same trousers. Black sack coat and vest. Act III: Black topcoat for funeral. For final scene: black ulster and gray hat over full black sack suit.

GEORGE—Act I. Tight gray checked woolen trousers. Peppermint striped shirt with high turnover collar and cuffs. Red bow tie. Black shoes. Act II. Dark blue trousers. Brown sweater. Brown striped turtle-necked dicky to permit under-dressing of white shirt. For wedding: same trousers with 4-button coat to match. White shirt and high turnover collar. Black tie (four-in-hand). Act III: Long black overcoat over wedding suit. Carry soft brown hat.

HOWIE NEWSOME—Act I. Blue overalls over old brown trousers. Heavy working shoes through-out play. Gray workshirt and gray sweater. Woolen cap (earmuff type). Act. II. Same. For wedding: tweed gray-brown suit. White shirt and collar. String tie. Brown felt hat. Act III. For funeral: long black coat and gray trousers, brown felt hat. For final scene: overalls with mackinaw. Same cap with earmuffs down. Mittens.

REBECCA—Act I. Blue checked gingham dress. Brown stockings. Black slippers. Blue hair-ribbon. Act II: (wedding). Tan and blue checked dress. Blue hair ribbon.

JOE CROWELL—Gray knickers. Brown sweater. Pink shirt. Brown shoes and long brown stockings.

PROF. WILLARD—Dark blue serge, shiny, double-breasted suit, coat unbuttoned. Black shoes. White collar and shirt. Black bow tie. Gold spectacles.

WOMAN IN BOX—Black street ensemble. Ponyskin cape. Gardenias. Black tricorne hat.

MAN IN AUDITORIUM—Dark business suit.

CONSTABLE WARREN—Throughout: Loose black suit. Black shoes. White shirt and collar. Dark tie. Gray felt hat worn flat. Spectacles.

SIMON STIMSON—Gray suit and tie. White shirt and high standing collar. Black shoes.

SI CROWELL—Long brown woolen pants. Brown sweater. Brown checked shirt open at neck. Brown shoes and gray socks.

SAM CRAIG—Black suit. Black silk socks. Black shoes. White shirt and turnover collar. Blue tie. Derby hat.

JOE STODDARD—Gray Prince Albert. White shirt and turnover collar. Black bow tie. Black shoes and socks. Black felt hat.

WALLY—Act I. Dark blue serge knickers. Blue shirt and blue bow tie. Black shoes and long black stockings. Act III. Same, with blue serge coat.

1ST BALLPLAYER—Old gray trousers. Blouse of gray baseball uniform. Black sneakers. Baseball glove.

2ND BALLPLAYER—Blue overalls. White torn shirt Black sweater around shoulders. Black sneakers. Baseball bat.

3RD BALLPLAYER—Brown trousers. Brown sweater. White shirt. Black sneakers. Baseball cap.

1ST DEAD MAN—Black Prince Albert. Standing collar. Black bow tie. Black shoes. Moustache.

2ND DEAD MAN—Black Prince Albert. Standing high collar. Black four-in-hand tie. Beard.

1ST DEAD WOMAN—Dark brown skirt. Figured brown waist. Black shoes and stockings.

2ND DEAD WOMAN—Brown tweed skirt. Green waist. Black shoes and stockings.

FARMER MCCARTHY—Black Prince Albert. Black shoes, stockings, four-in-hand. Wing collar.

EXTRAS—Men in dark colors throughout. Carry hats in wedding and funeral both. Women's skirts dark throughout. Waists colored for wedding, covered by dark capes and coats for funeral. Men wear dark coats for funeral.

PUBLICITY THROUGH YOUR LOCAL PAPERS

The press can be an immense help in giving publicity to your productions. In the belief that the best reviews from the New York and other large papers are always interesting to local audiences, and in order to assist you, we are printing below several excerpts from those reviews.

————

"One of the finest achievements of the current stage. Mr. Wilder has transmuted the simple events of a human life into universal reverie. He has given it a profound, strange, unworldly significance— brimming over with compassion. With about the best script of his career Mr. Harris has risen nobly to the occasion. In the staging he has appreciated the rare quality of Mr. Wilder's handiwork and illuminated it with a shining performance. 'Our Town' has escaped from the formal barrier of the modern theatre into the quintessence of acting, thought and speculation. A BEAUTIFULLY EVOCATIVE PLAY. A HAUNTINGLY BEAUTIFUL PLAY."   *New York Times*

————

"Clearly one of the events of the season—'Our Town' is both beautiful and touching."
New York Herald-Tribune

————

"There is no doubt that any season could count itself proud to bring forth 'Our Town'."
Robert Benchley, *The New Yorker*

————

"Mr. Wilder and Jed Harris have struck another blow at conventional theatre. 'Our Town' is a theatrical experience I would not like to miss. A beautiful and affecting play."

New York World-Telegram

" 'Our Town' reaches into the past of America and evokes movingly a way of life which is lost in our present turmoil. An original and extremely interesting play." *New York Sun*

"The first night audience was completely engrossed. Mr. Wilder has written with superb perception."

New York Journal-American

"A play of tremendous power. One of the great plays of our day."

New York Morning Telegraph

"It is the life of any town, of any human, from the cradle to the grave. It's really very fine."

Brooklyn Eagle

"A great play, worthy of an honored place in any anthology of the American drama. Performances to send the pulses racing, to put lumps in the throat."

New York Mirror

"One of the most important theatrical experiences of this generation. Wedding completely captures the essence of a million tearful weddings back home."

Chicago Tribune

"A supreme adventure in playgoing. If ever a play was predestined to live in the memory of an audience 'Our Town' is that play."

Chicago Journal of Commerce

"Reaches not only to your heart but often deep inside it. Frank Craven is as comfortable as an old shoe."

Chicago Herald and Examiner

"One of the best actors in the world, Frank Craven. A tipped hat to Jed Harris, who had the sand and imagination to cast and produce this fascinating 'script'."

Chicago American

"Superb in the writing, superb in the acting, superb in the staging, 'Our Town' is triply superb."

Chicago News

"Unconventional, intriguing. An absorbing experience in playgoing."

Chicago News

"In all my days as a theatregoer no play ever moved me so deeply."

Alexander Woollcott

"An exciting theatrical experience, moving in its drama, expressive in its philosophy, and fascinating in its technique."

Philadelphia Public Ledger

"Written with straightforward simplicity, sincerity and compassionate understanding—a play of rich and homely humanity."

Philadelphia Inquirer

"Nothing that has been said about it can quite match the charm and simplicity revealed in this little drama."

Philadelphia Evening Bulletin

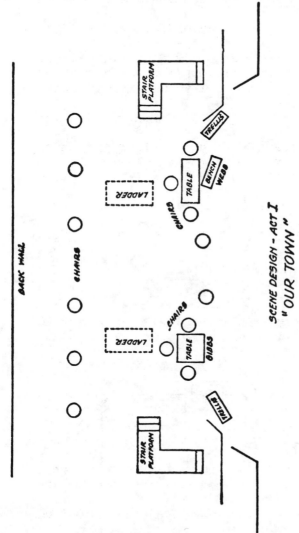

SCENE DESIGN - ACT I
"OUR TOWN"

99

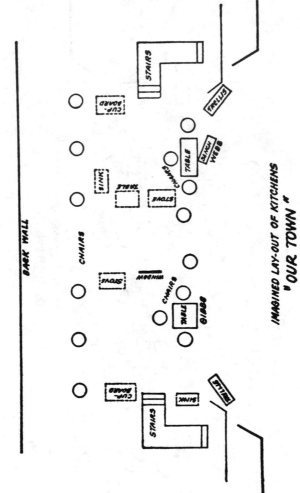

IMAGINED LAY-OUT OF KITCHENS
"OUR TOWN"

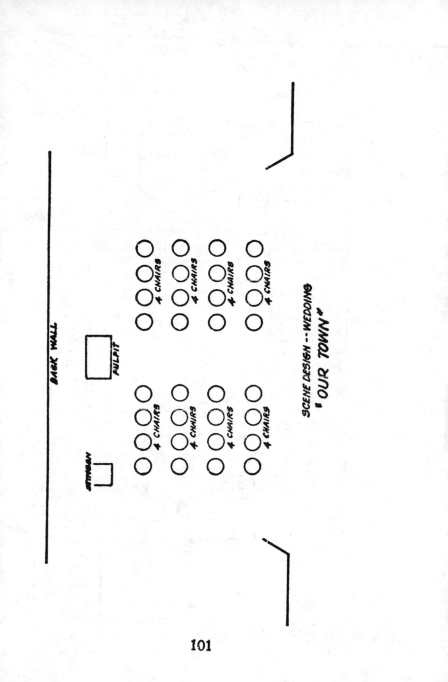

SCENE DESIGN -- WEDDING
"OUR TOWN"

101

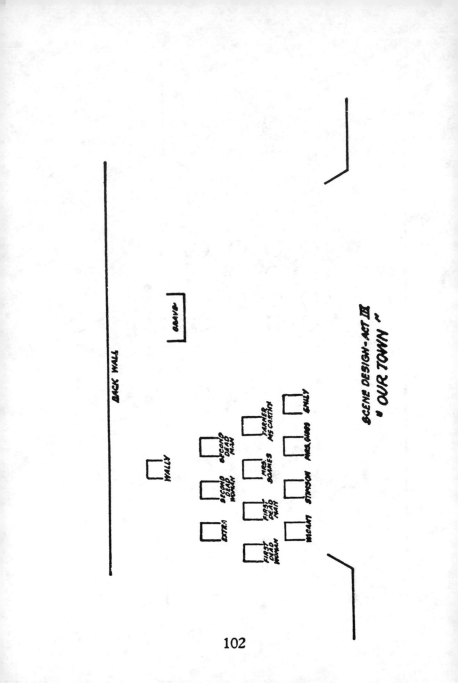

BACK WALL

GRAVE

WALLY

FIRST DEAD WOMAN

EXTRA

SECOND DEAD WOMAN

FIRST DEAD MAN

SECOND DEAD MAN

MRS. SOAMES

TURNER MS CARTHY

MR. GANT STIMSON MRS. GIBBS EMILY

SCENE DESIGN—ACT III
" OUR TOWN "

102